Science Art

Projects and Activities That Teach Science Concepts and Develop Process Skills

by Deborah Schecter

S C H O L A S T I C
PROFESSIONAL BOOKS

NEW YORK • TORONTO • LONDON • AUCKLAND • SYDNEY

*For my mother, Charlotte Bloch Schecter, who made art a natural part
of my childhood and who has always encouraged me
to imagine, explore, create, and grow.*

*For my father, Robert Schecter, and my aunt, Harriet Bloch Goldstone,
in loving memory.*

Heartfelt thanks to the following people
who helped me create this book:

JOAN NOVELLI, for polishing my manuscript with her expert editorial
eye and for adding so many valuable contributions.

KATHY MASSARO, for her elegant and exquisite design, and for going above
and beyond . . . as always.

DONNELLY MARKS, for her patience, good humor, and hilarious parrot story during our
very long photo shoot.

JAMES GRAHAM HALE, for his meticulous and lyrical artwork, and for always being
willing to create *just* one more piece of art.

FRAN NANKIN, LORI ANDRES, and MARIA CHANG, who worked with me at *SuperScience Red*
magazine, from which some of the projects in this book were adapted.

PETER COLÓN, who patiently stepped over and around jars of paint, paper
towel tubes, pipe cleaners, paper clips, and phone books filled with
pressed flowers, and lived with various concoctions on our
kitchen counters during the many months of testing
the projects in this book.

Edited by Joan Novelli
Science Consultant: Carolyn Sumners, Ed.D., Houston Museum of Natural Science
Cover and interior design by Kathy Massaro
Cover photos by Bob Lorenz
Interior photos by Donnelly Marks except: pages 31, 56–57, 73, 93, and 141 by Bob Lorenz; pages 12, 44, 62, 63, 86, and 98 by David Waitz; page 24 by Kimberly Butler; and page 29 by Camille Tokerud
Interior illustrations by James Graham Hale except: pages 19–20, and 42 by Ivy Rutzky; pages 14, 16, 20–21, 26, and 28 by Kate Flanagan; page 51 by Larry Daste; page 39 by Jeffrey Wiener; and page 92 by Maxie Chambliss

Contents

Sky Watch

Changes

Light, Color & Shadow

Exploring Energy 91

Forces & Movement 118

The Way Liquids Work 134

Introduction

Children are innately curious and creative, making them natural scientists and artists. When they delight in the colors of a rainbow after a sudden rain on a sunny day, admire the delicate symmetry of a butterfly's wings, or marvel at the way air moves to make wind chimes sing, they're discovering the science and art in the world around them—a world filled with invitations to investigate, create, and grow.

The activities in this collection are designed to help you bring the world of science and art into your classroom. Each activity is both a hands-on science investigation and an art experience. As students create satisfying art projects, they put science skills such as observing, predicting, investigating, and communicating to work too. While making inventive cards, toys, puppets, paintings, and other creations, abstract ideas become concrete and meaningful, helping students to see and understand the science around them.

The multifaceted nature of each activity will naturally appeal to a range of learning styles, nurturing students' strengths in all areas—from linguistic and logical-mathematical to intra- and interpersonal. Students will shine in the ways they learn best and at the same time have opportunities to discover new strengths and develop other areas. For example, as students create wind chimes (see Songs in the Wind, page 112), those with a special sensitivity to music

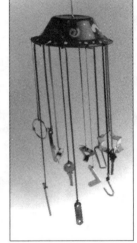

may be more aware of the sounds different materials make, while other students can use the experience to grow in this area. This same activity invites students to develop logical-mathematical thinking, too, as they look for patterns and relationships in the way the size, shape, and weight of various objects affect the sounds they make. And as students record impressions and responses in science journals, they'll strengthen linguistic abilities, painting pictures of their observations with words.

Support for the Science Standards

The projects in this book reflect the National Science Education Standards, the set of criteria intended to guide the quality of science teaching and learning in the United States. The standards outline important science content areas and support a hands-on, inquiry-based approach to learning. The first content standard, Science as Inquiry, applies to all of the activities in this book. This standard suggests that children ask questions, plan and carry out simple investigations, use tools to gather data, and communicate the results of their explorations. The chart on page 7 shows how the topics in this book correlate with other standards relating to content.

ScienceART Connections with the National Science Education Content Standards
Grades K–4

	PHYSICAL SCIENCE	EARTH & SPACE SCIENCE	LIFE SCIENCE	TECHNOLOGY
Plants & Seeds	objects have observable properties		organisms have basic needs; plants have structural parts that serve different functions	tools can be used to enhance observation; design process and products
Animal Adaptations	objects have observable properties		animals have body structures that serve different functions	design process and products
Sky Watch	heat moves through objects by conduction	objects in the sky have observable properties, locations, and patterns of movement; the sun gives light and heat; the moon's observable shape changes each month; changes in weather		tools can be used to enhance observation; design process and products
Changes	objects have observable properties; reactions between objects; changes in states of matter			design process and products
Light, Color & Shadow	properties of light; objects can reflect, refract, or absorb light			design process and products
Exploring Energy	objects have observable properties; electricity in circuits; heat moves by conduction; vibrating objects produce sound; factors that affect pitch	wind direction and speed		tools can be used to measure and enhance observation; design process and products
Forces & Movement	objects have observable properties; the position and motion of objects can be changed by pushes and pulls; magnets attract and repel each other and certain materials			tools can be used to enhance observation; design process and products
The Way Liquids Work	states of matter; objects have observable properties; position and motion of objects			tools can be used to measure; design process and products

A Look Inside

While nurturing their artistic talents with a variety of appealing projects, this book encourages students to explore science topics such as plants; animal adaptations; physical and chemical changes; light, color, and shadow; and magnetism. For example, in Crystal Chemistry (see page 56), students identify properties of solids and liquids, explore dissolving and evaporation, then record the changes they observe as they make sparkly, jewel-like decorations. In Painting with Plants (see page 22), students discover how plants use their colors—and how they can, too, to make beautiful bookmarks.

You can use *ScienceART* projects to introduce science concepts, to culminate particular science units you are teaching, or simply to introduce an art experience. Many projects connect with seasonal celebrations and other special holidays throughout the year. Students can create beautiful gifts and decorations for family and friends—and deepen their science understanding at the same time. Feel free to adapt a particular project as needed. For example, you can easily adapt the What Is Red? collage activity that invites students to explore the many variations of the color red for Valentine's Day (see page 71) to create color-collage cards for other holidays and seasonal themes. Students will also enjoy combining various projects such as using the iridescent paper they make (see Shimmery Color Bursts, page 81) to construct Starry Sky Mobiles (see page 123). You'll find suggestions for doing this throughout the book.

Each project in this book takes you from preparation to extensions. Here's an overview of what you'll find:

Science Talk

Background information explains science concepts and processes in easy-to-understand language. Feel free to adapt this information to meet the needs and abilities of your students.

Materials

A complete list of all materials and equipment needed for the project as well as possible substitutions.

Steps

Step-by-step directions suggest groupings for various activities, critical thinking questions to guide students' observations and investigations, and recording opportunities. In many cases, these directions also include exploratory activities to introduce students to key science concepts.

Tips

Helpful management tips and ideas for enhancements to help make projects go smoothly.

Book Breaks

Suggested fiction and nonfiction books that connect with the topic. You'll note that many of these are picture books. Because they explain science concepts in clear, easy-to-understand language, you'll find them useful for children of all ages.

Variations and Extensions

Suggestions for altering the basic project or for exploring other variables, plus additional projects and activities that link curriculum areas such as language arts, math, or social studies.

Reproducible Patterns

Give students a head start on some of the projects with patterns they can cut out and use.

Reproducible Science Journal Pages

Ready-to-use journal pages, included for many activities, emphasize process skills and help students organize their data. Students can add these pages to their science journals. (See Setting up Science Journals, below.)

Setting up Science Journals

Science journals are an important part of any inquiry-based science program. A personal journal gives each student a place to respond to and ask questions and to reflect on science activities. Writing about and drawing pictures of observations, predictions, and results helps students develop process skills such as communicating and recording data. In addition, they'll be able to track the results of ongoing investigations and changes they observe over time. (For example, the variables that affect the spinning power of a pinwheel or the changing appearance of a carved apple face as it dries.)

Science journals can also help you to assess how well students grasp certain concepts and evaluate growth in various process skills such as observing and predicting. For example, do students' drawings reflect more detail over time? Are they labeled and sequenced correctly? Do students incorporate new science vocabulary in their entries and explain the reasons for their predictions? You'll also be able to use the journals to encourage students' writing skills, for example, focusing on specific language and detailing the steps in a process.

Science journals can be loose-leaf notebooks that students add pages to as needed, along with the reproducible journal pages in this book. (Provide a hole punch for students to use or prepunch these pages.) To make their own science journals, students can fold a 12-by-18-inch piece of tagboard in half, mark and punch holes (to fit standard notebook paper), add pages, and bind with brass paper fasteners, ribbon, string, or O rings. Invite students to decorate the covers with projects from this book such as Leafprint Book Covers (see page 14), Pressed Flower Projects (see page 21), or Marbleized Paper Pictures (see page 135).

Supply Sources

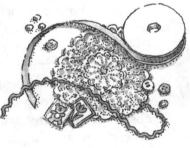

Save, save, save! Scraps of construction paper, bits of felt, gift wrappings and ribbons, jars of different shapes and sizes—all of these will come in handy. Most of the projects in this book use materials that are low cost and easy to collect. Many use items you can recycle, such as paper towel tubes, old file folders, and empty food containers. If you have room, designate a corner of your classroom to hold labeled boxes or baskets of different kinds of materials. When you or your students need a particular item (or are looking for creative inspiration), you can check the appropriate box or basket to find what you need.

Sources for additional materials:

For arts-and-crafts supplies, such as wiggly eyes, beads, felt, pipe cleaners, decorative papers, glitter, and sequins:
Oriental Trading Co. (800) 228-2269
S & S Crafts (800) 243-9232
Sax Arts & Crafts (800) 558-6696

For magnets, mirrors, batteries, bulbs, and other science supplies:
Delta Education (800) 258-1302
Edmund Scientific (609) 547-8880
The Magnet Source (800) 525-3536
Radio Shack (800) 223-8344

Groupings and Work Areas

Directions for each activity offer grouping suggestions. Some activities work best when children work on their own; others are set up for cooperative group work in which students share materials and brainstorm ideas about their investigations. To guide participation in group activities, you may wish to assign each child a different task, such as gather materials, keep records, investigate, and report findings.

If time is short, consider spreading some activities over several days, or invite students to take their projects home to finish with a family member. You'll find that many projects are suitable for learning center setups too, allowing students to help one another and share observations and results. Stock the center with necessary materials, post directions, and review the steps of the activity with students ahead of time. If activities include introductory demonstrations of science concepts, plan to do these with the class before having students work on their own at the center.

Tips for Managing Activities

❂ Try to test each project before doing it with students. This will help you identify needed materials and assess the amount of time you'll need, including time for setup and cleanup. Doing the project yourself will also help prepare you to guide students through the project. Jot down notes for yourself, including questions you might ask at different stages in the process.

❂ To make setup, distribution, and cleanup go smoothly, organize materials in labeled containers on a large table. Have trays available to students for collecting materials.

❂ Have smocks and plenty of old newspapers and paper towels on hand for messy activities.

❂ Allow plenty of time for questions. Encourage students to share observations, discoveries, tips, problems, and solutions with classmates as they work. If students have their own theories, try to find time for testing them and sharing results. Before wrapping up an activity, bring students together for a class discussion.

A Note About Safety

The projects in this book use materials that are safe for children to handle. However, adult supervision is recommended for all projects. Directions for several activities include special safety notes, for example, reminding you to have students wash hands after handling certain materials or avoid looking directly at the sun. Please use your discretion if you plan to have students do any of the activities on their own. When sending activities home, include a note suggesting that an adult family member do the activity with the child.

ScienceART on Display

Students will take great pride in displaying their *ScienceART* projects in a prominent place. Here are some ideas for displaying students' work.

☀ Let each child design a display space as part of a larger bulletin board. Invite students to share work they're most proud of, changing their own displays as they create new projects.

☀ Loan a collection of student work for display to a local business, the school or public library, or the front office. Have students make tags to display with their work, providing their names and other pertinent information. Rotate the display periodically.

☀ Plan a *ScienceART* fair and invite other classes and family members to visit. Include students' science journals and encourage children to share them with visitors.

Frameable Art

☀ For the simplest frame, fold construction paper or tagboard in half as shown and cut out a window, leaving a frame of about one to two inches. Enhance the basic frame by cutting interior or exterior borders. Decorate with scraps of lace, ribbon, rickrack, or pieces of cut-up paper doilies.

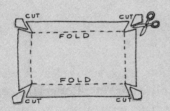 

☀ For a three-dimensional look, clip the corners of the frame, bend the edges up as shown, and tape in place from the back. Attach art from the back of the frame, taping or gluing it to the top, bottom, and sides.

☀ To make round frames, cut out the center of a paper plate, then paint and decorate the outer edge. Glue artwork to the back. Punch a hole in a small piece of cardboard and attach to the back to make a hanger. This type of frame is a beautiful way to display pressed leaf and flower projects. (See pages 17 and 21.)

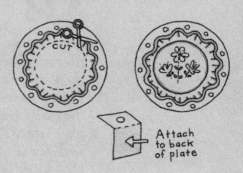

Plants & Seeds

From tall trees with widespread branches that reach for the sky to tiny flowers that hug the ground, plants come in many sizes, shapes, and colors. Explore plants and how they grow with the projects in this chapter. Students can collaborate on a tree collage, design leafprint book covers, make pressed flower projects, and more—sharpening their observation and prediction skills in the process.

Build a Tree

Students put together branches, twigs, and other tree parts they find to discover more about how trees grow.

Materials

A Tree Is Growing (optional)
grocery bags (1 per student pair)
tree parts (leaves, seeds, twigs, branches, bark)
bulletin board paper
glue or tape
pushpins or tacks
brown crayons, markers, yarn, or construction paper

SCIENCE TALK

Trees have five main parts: roots, bark, trunk, leaves, and seeds. Each helps a tree in a different way. Roots anchor a tree to the ground. Tiny root hairs grow at the tips of smaller roots, absorbing water and minerals from the soil. The roots of a large apple tree can absorb as much as 95 gallons of water in one day! Bark protects a tree. An inner layer carries nutrients from leaves to other parts of the tree. The outer layer is made up of dead tissue from the inner bark. The trunk is the tree's stem. It carries nutrients and water from the soil to other tree parts and holds up the leafy branches to get sunlight. Leaves are a tree's food makers, the place where photosynthesis takes place. How do new trees grow? Tree seeds scatter and take root. Some seeds, like maple, have wings that propel them to the ground. Animals like birds and squirrels help scatter seeds too, by eating a tree's fruit and dropping the seeds as they travel.

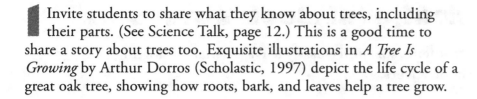

1 Invite students to share what they know about trees, including their parts. (See Science Talk, page 12.) This is a good time to share a story about trees too. Exquisite illustrations in *A Tree Is Growing* by Arthur Dorros (Scholastic, 1997) depict the life cycle of a great oak tree, showing how roots, bark, and leaves help a tree grow.

2 Take students outside to collect tree parts such as branches, twigs, leaves, and bark from the ground. Discuss the importance of respecting living things. Ask: Why do you think it's not okay to pull parts off trees? Guide students to understand that a tree's parts help it grow. Pulling off parts hurts the tree. Have students work in pairs and share collecting bags.

TIP If possible, do this activity after rainy or windy weather, when tree parts may have been blown to the ground. If students can't find fallen pieces of bark, they can make bark rubbings by holding paper to a tree, then firmly rubbing a brown crayon on its side across the paper. (Plan ahead and bring these materials with you on the walk.)

3 Back inside, invite students to sort tree parts into groups (leaves, branches, twigs, seeds, and so on). Then have them use the parts to create a tree collage. Encourage students first to plan their design on the floor. Then cover a bulletin board with paper and have students use glue, tape, or pushpins to put up the tree parts.

4 Invite students to label the parts of their tree. What parts are missing? They probably didn't find unattached roots outside, so let students make their own with brown crayons or markers, yarn, or construction paper.

BOOK BREAK

Enrich students' explorations by sharing *The Tree* by Judy Hindley (Clarkson N. Potter, 1990). Each double-page spread features a simple poem about a different kind of tree with lyrical text that tells more.

Follow up by taking a close look at one tree in *Sky Tree*, written and illustrated by Thomas Locker (HarperCollins, 1995). This book, with splendid paintings that show the changes of one tree, will inspire children to keep their own picture journals of a favorite tree they observe over time. Use the author's notes in the back to show students how they can create the effects they want, for example, blending blue and white to create a soft summer sky, or using muted colors to show a late autumn tree's fading colors.

Leafprint Book Covers

Students sort and classify leaves to make colorful book covers.

Materials

large plastic bags (1 per student)
assorted fresh leaves
craft paper
scissors
newspaper
tempera paint
paintbrushes or cut-up sponges
tape
rolling pins or soup cans (optional)

TIP If you live in an area where leaves turn colors and fall off trees in autumn, this is a perfect time to plan this activity. Any time of the year will do, though. You'll want to prepare for this activity by creating a sample book cover. Gather a few leaves of your own and use them to print designs on a book cover pattern. (See step 4.)

1 Give each student a plastic bag and take a leaf-collecting walk. Reinforce respect for living things by discussing reasons for picking up leaves from the ground rather than taking them off trees. (See Science Talk, page 12.) Encourage students to look carefully at the shapes and colors of the leaves they see and to collect as many different types as they can. Flat leaves without holes or curled edges will work best.

Leaf Types

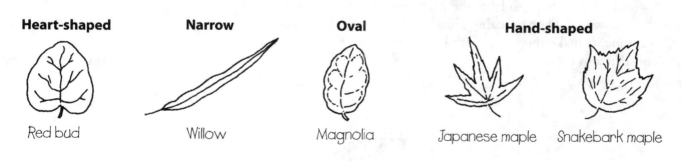

Heart-shaped
Red bud

Narrow
Willow

Oval
Magnolia

Hand-shaped
Japanese maple   Snakebark maple

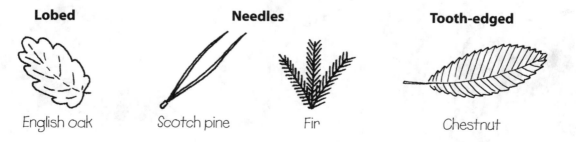

Lobed
English oak

Needles
Scotch pine   Fir

Tooth-edged
Chestnut

2 Back in class, divide students into groups to study and sort leaves by attributes such as color, size, shape (number of lobes, edge type, broad-leaf or needle-like), vein pattern, and so on. You might have students use Venn diagrams to classify the leaves in different ways. Use the leaf charts on pages 14 and 16 as reference.

3 Bring the class together to share findings. Compile a chart of leaf characteristics.

4 Guide students in cutting out paper for book covers, using the illustration here as reference and resizing to fit assorted books as needed. Invite students to use their leaves to print designs on their book covers. (Have a sample printed book cover on hand to share.)

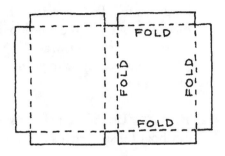

- Spread newspaper on a work surface. Gather paints and brushes or sponges.

- Plan leaf arrangement, for example using several leaves in a repeating pattern, or a few of the characteristics listed on the chart.

- Practice brushing paint over the vein side of a leaf's surface and pressing it paint side down onto newspaper. Place a piece of scrap paper over the leaf and rub the paper firmly. (A rolling pin or a heavy can is useful for this part.) Gently lift up the paper and peel off the leaf.

- Use the same technique to make leafprints on the book cover. (Students might choose shades of green, or red, orange, and yellow to capture the colors of autumn.)

TIP The waxy surface of some leaves may prevent paint from sticking evenly. If this happens, add a drop of dishwashing liquid to the paint. For more clearly defined prints, use acrylic paints.

5 When the paint dries, show students how to fold and tape their book covers around a book. These make wonderful covers for science journals!

- **GIFT WRAP:** Unroll bulletin board paper on the floor. Cover with leafprints, then cut in gift-wrap size sections and distribute.

- **NOTE CARDS:** Use small leaves to make prints on 5-by-8-inch unlined index cards folded in half. Decorate envelopes with leafprints too. For a special gift, make sets of cards and envelopes, wrap in leafprint gift wrap (above), and tie up with green ribbon or yarn.

- **T-SHIRTS:** Use fabric paint instead of tempera and put a piece of cardboard inside each shirt to keep the paint from soaking through.

- **NEGATIVE SPACE PRINTS:** Roll pieces of tape so the sticky side faces out and use these to attach leaves to paper. Paint around leaves, working out from the leaf edges. When the paint dries, remove the leaves.

- **LEAF RUBBINGS:** Tape a flat leaf with prominent veins on a flat surface. Then tape a piece of tissue paper or tracing paper over the leaf. Rub a dark-colored crayon back and forth, in the same direction, across the paper.

Leaf Vein Patterns

Pinnate

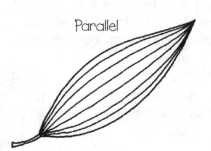

Parallel

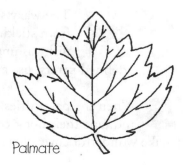

Palmate

Pressed Leaf Place Mats

These see-through place mats show off leaf patterns beautifully.

Materials

assorted leaves
telephone books
heavy books, bricks, or other weights
paper towels
newspaper
waxed paper, cut into 18-inch lengths (2 pieces per student)
crayon shavings (use an old cheese grater to make crayon shavings easily)
iron
ribbon, rickrack, or colored tape
glue

1 Have students place leaves they've collected between the pages of thick telephone books, first placing the leaves between paper towels to absorb excess moisture. Put heavy books, a few bricks, or other heavy weights on top. In about two or three weeks, the leaves will be dry and flat.

2 Set up a work center in a corner of your room near an electrical outlet. Put a thick layer of newspaper on the work surface to protect it from the heat of the iron.

3 Have students take turns laying one piece of waxed paper on the newspaper and arranging leaves on it, leaving at least a one-inch border around the edges. Let students sprinkle crayon shavings around their leaves, then place a second piece of waxed paper on top, lining up the edges carefully.

4 Place several sheets of newspaper on top of the waxed paper, then iron (adult only) for one to two minutes, using a warm setting.

5 Remove the newspaper. The melted crayon enhances the leaf designs and holds the waxed paper together. Have students cut off uneven edges of the paper and trim the borders with ribbon, rickrack, or colored tape. A set of place mats makes a wonderful gift for parents or grandparents!

BOOK BREAK

Share with students how various poets view green life on Earth in *The Earth Is Painted Green: A Garden of Poems About Our Planet* edited by Barbara Brenner (Scholastic, 1994). Divided into chapters such as "First Green," "Planting Green," "Harvest Green," and "Last Green," readers follow the year-round cycle of growing things.

STAINED-GLASS LEAF ART: Make smaller pressed leaf mats, cutting waxed paper into rectangles, squares, or circles. Punch a hole at the top of the design, tie a ribbon through the hole, and hang in a window. Or combine several for a beautiful sunlit effect.

LEAFY CRITTERS: Explore the physical characteristics of leaves to make imaginative leaf critters. Start by looking at leaves. What animal parts do the different leaves suggest? (Long, thin leaves might make a jackrabbit's ears; a fan-shaped ginkgo leaf, a whale's tail or the frill on a triceratops's head; a cluster of pine needles might make a squirrel's tail or a horse's mane; and so on.) Invite students to use pressed leaves to create leafy critters and glue them onto construction paper. Display designs on a Leafy-Critter Zoo bulletin board. Can anyone guess what the animals are?

Pollinators at Work

Students make model flowers and demonstrate how cross-pollination takes place.

Materials

flower petal and bee patterns (page 20)
brightly colored construction paper
scissors
hole punch
plastic straws (1 per student)
1 yellow and 4 green pipe cleaners (per student)
tape
cornmeal

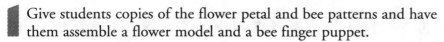

1 Give students copies of the flower petal and bee patterns and have them assemble a flower model and a bee finger puppet.

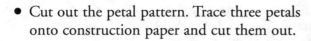

- Cut out the petal pattern. Trace three petals onto construction paper and cut them out.

- Stack the petals together and use the hole punch to make a hole in the middle. To enhance the flowery effect, crease the petals lengthwise and crosswise.

- Push the straw through the holes and spread out the petals. If the petals slide down the straw, wrap a bit of tape around the straw, just under the petals.

- Stick four green pipe cleaners and one yellow pipe cleaner into the straw, bending or curling each slightly at the tip.

- Cut out the bee finger puppet, wrap it around the end of your index finger, and ask a classmate to tape it in place.

BOOK BREAK

The bold illustrations and playful verse in *The Reason for a Flower* by Ruth Heller (Grosset & Dunlap, 1983) help explain how the interdependence of animals and plants aids in plant reproduction.

Another book that explores this theme is *Jack's Garden* by Henry Cole (Greenwillow, 1995). Soft, detailed color-pencil illustrations of wildflowers, insects, and other garden creatures enhance the text, written in a "House That Jack Built" formula.

2 Have students study their flowers. Ask: What do you think the *petals* do? Guide students to understand that the petals protect the other flower parts. Their bright colors also attract insects such as bees and butterflies, and they in turn help the flower make seeds through a process called *pollination*. Then explain that the green pipe cleaners represent the *stamens*—the parts of the flower that make pollen and the yellow pipe cleaner the *pistil*—the part where seeds grow.

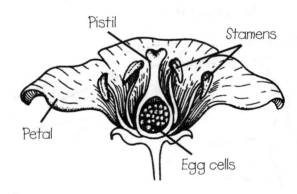

3 Walk around the room and sprinkle some pollen (cornmeal) on the stamens of each student's flower. Then, wearing their bee finger puppets, have students work in pairs to cross-pollinate each other's flowers. Each bee visits her or his own flower, picks up some pollen between the index finger and thumb, then visits the partner's flower and drops some pollen on that flower's pistil. (In nature, pistils are often sticky so they will hold onto pollen. You can moisten the pipe cleaner pistils with water or a bit of honey to simulate this.)

TIP Students can add pipe cleaner legs to their bees and use them instead of their fingers to pollinate one another's flowers.

Sweet Sachets: Besides their bright petals, the fragrance of flowers also helps to attract the insects that pollinate them. Capture this fragrance by making potpourri sachets. Collect flower petals from roses, honeysuckle, apple blossoms, lily of the valley, peonies, and other fragrant flowers. (You might ask local florists for donations of old flowers.)

- Spread petals on a screen. Place the screen between two chairs so air can circulate. Set in a warm place, away from direct sunlight.

- Turn petals regularly as they dry over the next few weeks.

- Put small amounts of the petals in jars or fabric or cheesecloth squares and tie with a colorful ribbon. Store unused petals in sealed plastic bags.

Flower petal pattern

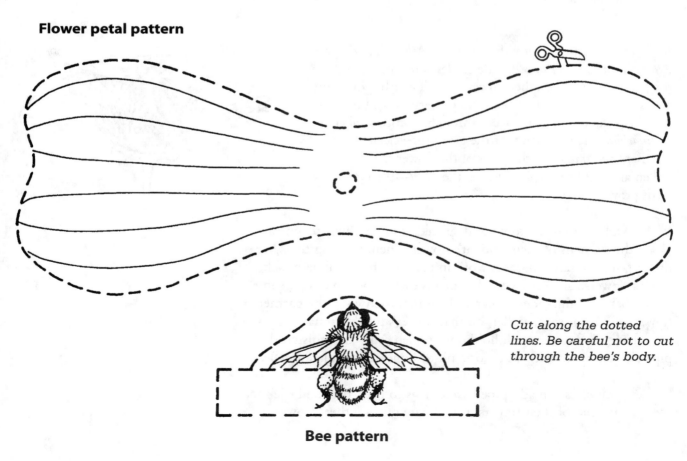

Cut along the dotted lines. Be careful not to cut through the bee's body.

Bee pattern

Pressed Flower Projects

Children become budding botanists as they identify and collect flowers and then use them in pressed flower projects.

SCIENCE TALK

Fringed gentians, white milkweed, showy lady's slipper, and Indian paintbrush are just some of the wildflowers that are endangered. Reasons for their endangered status include loss of habitat (for example, fields that have been turned into parking lots or building sites) as well as pollution of land and water. Contact your state Department of Natural Resources for more information about endangered flowers in your area. Invite children to find and share pictures of these flowers.

Showy lady's slipper   White milkweed   Indian paintbrush   Fringed gentian

Materials

assorted small wildflowers such as violets, yarrow, forget-me-nots, and buttercups
Wildflower Finder journal page (page 27)
wildflower field guide (see Book Break, page 22)

1 Take students on a flower-collecting field trip. Have them bring along several copies of the Wildflower Finder journal page. When collecting flowers to press, take along a field guide to help identify different varieties and avoid picking any endangered species. (See Science Talk, above.) Remind students to pick only what they need and not to pull up flowers by their roots. Also, don't pick flowers with hard or fleshy centers, because they will be difficult to flatten and do not press well. As students discover flowers, have them record observations on their wildflower charts.

2 Back in the classroom, press the flowers as soon as possible (see Pressed Leaf Place Mats for directions and materials, page 17), saving a few samples of each type for students to study.

3 Have students examine the samples and compare their appearance, scent, and texture, then identify the flowers' parts. (See Pollinators at Work, page 18.)

4 When the pressed flowers are ready, have students use them in art projects. (See Variations, below.)

• • • VARIATIONS • • •

NAPKIN RINGS: Cut paper towel tubes into 2-inch rings and paint. Dab glue onto the back of the flowers and attach to the rings. Add leaves and grasses for variety. Cover with contact paper, rubbing firmly to press out air bubbles. Trim off excess. Glue ribbon, rickrack, or other trim to the edges. Use the same technique to make tagboard bookmarks, cards, and gift tags.

WINDOW HANGINGS: Press flowers between sheets of waxed paper (see page 17), put in construction paper frames, and hang in a window.

PENCIL HOLDERS: Wrap a piece of construction paper around a clean, empty soup can. (Check for sharp edges first.) Tape it in place and trim off excess. Glue on pressed flowers, small leaves, ferns, and grasses. Cover with contact paper.

Painting with Plants

Students explore the natural pigments in plants as they make beautiful bookmarks.

▲ ▲ ▲ SCIENCE TALK ▲ ▲ ▲

The colors in flowers and other plants serve different purposes in nature. Chlorophyll in leaves gives them their green color and plays an important role in how plants manufacture food through photosynthesis. Colorful flowers attract insects to help in the process of pollination. Colorful fruits attract animals to eat them and help spread their seeds.

Materials

assorted plant parts (see Tip, below)

Painting with Plants journal page (page 28)

plastic sandwich bags

muslin or old white cotton pillowcases or sheets cut into 2-by-8-inch strips,
  (use pinking shears or scalloped scissors for a more interesting effect)
  (1 per student)

cotton swabs (optional)

TIP When preparing for this activity, you might want to ask at florists' shops, garden centers, and grocery stores for flowers, vegetables, fruits, and other plants that would otherwise be thrown away. Send a note home requesting donations. (For odor control, you may want to plan a day to collect and experiment with these.) Plant parts that work well include geranium petals, grass cuttings, spinach leaves, berries, grapes, tea leaves, coffee grounds, parsley, onion skins, and red cabbage leaves.

1 Place a few pieces of each plant in a plastic bag. Label each bag with the plant's name.

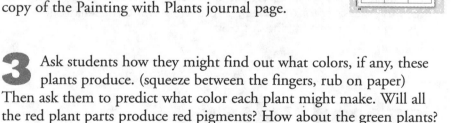

2 Divide students into groups. Give each group a few bags of plant samples and each student a copy of the Painting with Plants journal page.

3 Ask students how they might find out what colors, if any, these plants produce. (squeeze between the fingers, rub on paper) Then ask them to predict what color each plant might make. Will all the red plant parts produce red pigments? How about the green plants? After recording plant names and guesses, have students test the plant parts by rubbing them on their science journal pages.

4 Bring students together to share their discoveries. What plants produced surprising colors?

5 Let students use the fabric strips and plant pigments to make colorful bookmarks. Cotton swabs are useful for rubbing plant pigments into the cloth. (Have students make sure the pigments are dry before using the bookmarks in books.)

BOOK BREAK

A New Coat for Anna by Harriet Ziefert (Knopf, 1986), set in wartime Europe, tells the story of a young girl and her mother who barter for the materials they need to make a new coat and use natural dyes to color the fabric.

To encourage students to take a closer look at nature's colors, share *The Legend of the Indian Paintbrush* by Tomie dePaola (Putnam, 1988), the story of a young Native American boy who spends his days trying to make colors as beautiful as those in the sunset. He finally realizes his dream in a tale that explains how the Indian paintbrush flower was named.

• • • E X T E N S I O N S • • •

Plant Impressions: Place several folded sheets of newspaper inside a cotton T-shirt. Place the T-shirt on a surface you can hammer on, such as a wooden board. Arrange leaves facedown on the front of the shirt. (Delicate leaves with thin stems such as ferns work best.) Lay a piece of waxed paper over the leaves and then pound the leaves evenly and firmly, until an imprint appears. When the shirt is washed, the color will fade, leaving a delicate impression.

Nature's Colors: Research ways people long ago used natural dyes from plants. For example, in Colonial America, people used flowers, leaves, roots, bark, nutshells, and berries to color the yarn or fabrics they made into clothing. Experiment with using some of these materials to dye fabric. (See How Heat Helps, below.)

How Heat Helps: Explore the effect of heat in releasing plant pigments. Fill a reclosable plastic bag with about 1/4 cup of warm water. Add about 2 tablespoons of plant parts (such as crushed onion skins, grated beets or red cabbage, spinach leaves, or ground spices such as paprika and cumin). Squish the plant matter inside the bag for a few minutes. What happens to the water? (Pigments from the plants color the water.) Experiment using these liquid dyes to color different kinds of cloth.

Egghead Pals

Students investigate what seeds need to sprout by growing plant pals.

Materials
eggshell halves, washed (1 per student plus 4 extras)
seeds (radish, grass, or alfalfa)
cotton balls
measuring spoons
empty egg cartons
soil
water
cardboard
paper strips, about 1 by 5 inches (1 per student)
tape
markers

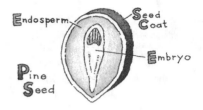

SCIENCE TALK

Seeds contain all the parts a plant needs to *germinate* or begin to grow. The outer seed coat protects the plant embryo (the baby plant) within from harm. The seed also contains a built-in food supply (either an endosperm or cotyledon depending on the type of seed). This food supply sustains the growing plant until it can manufacture its own food through photosynthesis. So initially plants don't need soil, light, or nutrients to germinate—just water, air, and a place to grow. After a plant has sprouted and the seed's food supply is depleted, it relies on nutrients in soil and the sun for photosynthesis.

In this activity, eggshells make good short-term planters because they hold their shape but are slightly porous. As the plants grow, their roots will need more room. To replant, gently poke holes in the shells, then put them into a larger pot or the ground. The eggshells, made of calcium carbonate, will break down (and even help improve the quality of the soil by making it more alkaline).

1 Let students examine some seeds and draw pictures of them in their science journals. Then guide students in planting their eggshells.

- Place a few cotton balls in the shell.

- Sprinkle a pinch (about 1/8 teaspoon) of seeds into the shell. Cover them with a bit of cotton.

- Set the shell in the egg carton.

- Write your name outside the egg carton cup in which your shell is sitting.

2 Now invite students to help you plant eggshells for a scientific comparison.

- Place cotton balls in three extra shells. Set the eggshells in an egg carton. Add seeds to each and cover with a bit of cotton. Label one "no water," one "too much water," and one "no light."

- Fill a fourth shell halfway with soil and set it in the carton. (This is the *control* or basis for comparison.) Sprinkle a pinch of seeds in the shell. Cover them with a bit of soil.

- Saturate the cotton in the "too much water" shell with water. Add a teaspoon of water to the shell labeled "no light" and cover it with a piece of cardboard. Add a teaspoon of water to the shell filled with soil.

3 Ask students to predict and record which seeds they think will sprout. Will the seeds without soil sprout? Those with no water or too much water? How about those without light?

4 Have students make daily observations of the seeds and record changes in their science journals. Ask: How have the seeds changed since yesterday? What parts of the plant can you see? What happened to the seed coats? When the cotton or soil feels dry, add water to all but the "no water" shell. Make sure the "too much water" shell stays soaked.

5 In a few days, the seeds in all the shells except for the "no water" and "too much water" shell should grow hairlike sprouts. When this happens, ask: What do you think seeds need to germinate? (Seeds need just air, moisture, and a place to grow. Overwatering the seeds in one of the shells drives out air, which prevents the plant from growing.)

6 To complete their egghead pals, have students decorate the paper strips, then tape them into circles as shown (making necks for their eggheads to rest on). Invite students to use markers to draw faces on their eggheads.

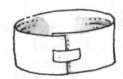

• • • • VARIATION • • • •

GROW PLANT PICTURES: Use a pencil to poke a few holes in the bottom of a foil cake pan. Pat about one inch of soil into the pan. Plan a plant picture design (initials, a heart, and so on). Trace the design into the soil (about 1/2 inch deep), then drop in seeds. Sprinkle soil over the seeds and pat down. Place the pan on a tray in a sunny spot. Keep the soil moist and watch for the picture to appear!

• • • EXTENSION • • •

Mushroom Spore Prints: Mushrooms are a type of fungus, like mold and yeast. (They lack chlorophyll and do not produce their own food as green plants do.) Instead of seeds, mushrooms grow from spores, contained in finlike gills. To make spore prints, gather or purchase a variety of fresh mushrooms. (Remind students never to taste any wild mushrooms they find.) Cut off the stems and peel away the rounded part of the cap that curves inward. Place the mushrooms gill side down on construction paper (light-colored paper for dark gills, dark-colored for light gills). Place the papers in an area where they won't be disturbed and cover the caps with jars or bowls. The next day, carefully remove the coverings and lift the mushrooms straight up off the paper. Spores that have fallen out of the gills leave circular prints on the paper. To preserve the prints, spray them lightly with hair spray in a well-ventilated area.

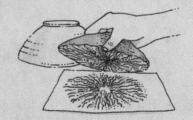

Wildflower Finder

Name _____

Draw a picture below of a wildflower you see.

Describe the place you found it.

_____

_____

Record the number of flowers on the stem. _____

Draw a picture of a leaf on the stem. Describe the leaf edge.

How many pistils does each flower on the stem have? _____

How many stamens do you see? _____

If you know the flower's name, write it here.

_____

Name _____

Painting with Plants

▲▲▲▲▲▲▲▲▲▲▲▲

What color will each plant make?
Make a prediction. Then test each plant.

Plant Name	My Prediction	Results

Animal Adaptations

What makes insects different from other kinds of bugs? How do colors and body coverings keep animals safe? Why is a delicate-looking bird's nest so durable? With the activities in this chapter, students create art projects that explore the adaptations and behaviors that make animals unique and help them survive.

Edible Insects

Students make candy models to learn the basic parts of an insect.

SCIENCE TALK

Insects belong to a group of animals called *arthropods*. These creatures have jointed legs, segmented bodies, and no backbone. Most insects have six legs and three main body parts: the head, the thorax, and the abdomen. Eyes, antennae, and mouthparts are on the head. Legs and wings are attached to the thorax. Instead of bones, insects have an exoskeleton, a shell-like skeleton that protects their bodies. Spiders have eight legs, two body parts (an abdomen and head), and no antennae. These arthropods belong to a group of animals called *arachnids*. Earthworms have segmented bodies with a band called a clitellum. Earthworms belong to a group of animals called *annelids*.

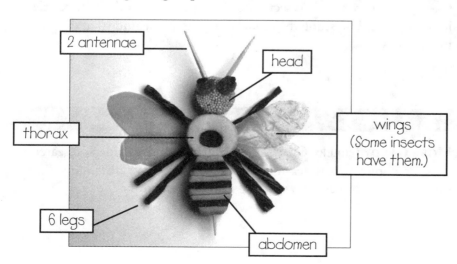

2 antennae

head

thorax

wings
(Some insects have them.)

6 legs

abdomen

Young scientists will enjoy these books about insects and other creepy crawly bugs.

- *Backyard Bugs* by Robin Kittrell Laughlin (Chronicle Books, 1996) has fabulous full-color photos of 65 different bugs, including many insects. Fascinating background information tells about each creature.

- *Bugs* by Nancy Winslow Parker and Joan Richards Wright (Greenwillow, 1987). Labeled diagrams accompany soft illustrations of 16 different bugs. Humorous riddles complement the informative text.

- *Flit! Flutter! Fly!* poems selected by Lee Bennett Hopkins (Doubleday, 1992) is a poetry collection custommade for choral reading. Inviting illustrations enhance these 20 "buggy" tributes.

Materials

pictures or photos of insects

assorted soft candy in different shapes (such as gumdrops, mini-marshmallows shoestring licorice, fruit leather, jelly beans)

toothpicks (colored ones make a great effect)

Insect Key journal page (page 41)

TIP Instead of candy, you can substitute arts-and-crafts materials such as pipe cleaners, foam packing pieces, colored cellophane, and waxed paper or different kinds of vegetables such as cauliflower florets, carrot circles, cherry tomatoes, green beans, zucchini slices, and mushrooms.

1 Invite students to study pictures or photos of insects such as butterflies, grasshoppers, beetles, dragonflies, ants, and bees. Ask: What do these insects have in common? Hand out the Insect Key journal page and explain that every insect has the parts shown.

2 Distribute bowls containing assorted kinds of candy and toothpicks. Invite students to use the materials to make insects (real or imaginary). Guide them by asking questions.

- How many pieces will you need to make an insect's body? (Encourage students to check the Insect Key. They can use toothpicks to hold the body parts together.)

- How many toothpicks will you add to make legs and antennae? Where on the body do they go?

- Does your insect have wings? If so, what can you use to make them?

3 When students are finished, have them describe how they constructed their insects and draw pictures on their Insect Key journal pages. Use students' models to assess their understanding of insect parts.

● ● ● ● V A R I A T I O N ● ● ● ●

MORE CANDY CREEPY CRAWLIES: Construct candy spiders, researching these arachnids first to learn about their parts. How are spiders different from insects? Try making candy earthworms too.

Butterfly Symmetry

Students explore symmetry in nature by making bright butterflies.

Look closely at a butterfly's wings and you'll see that each is made up of thousands of overlapping, iridescent scales—a shining example of symmetry in nature. A line of symmetry divides a shape into two identical parts. In some cases, as with a butterfly, you'll find one line of symmetry. In other cases, there is more than one—as with the eight sections of an orange.

Materials

books about butterflies (see Book Break, page 32)
old newspapers
round coffee filters or paper towels cut into 9-inch circles (1 per student)
food coloring in squeeze bottles (several sets)
plastic cups (1 per student)
water
spring-type clothespins (1 per student)
pipe cleaners
wiggly eyes and glue (optional)
smocks

1 Gather assorted books about butterflies and let students get together in small groups to read about these colorful insects and study the patterns on their wings. Bring students together after a while to discuss how the patterns are useful to butterflies (camouflage, alert predators that the butterfly is poison, attract a mate).

2 Ask students to describe characteristics many butterflies have in common (bright colors, distinctive markings and patterns, wings are the mirror image of each other).

3 Invite students to create their own butterflies. First cover work surfaces with newspapers. Divide students into groups. Give each group bottles of food coloring to share. Each student will need a cup of water and a coffee filter.

4 Show students how to fold the coffee filter in half, then in half again. Demonstrate how to dab designs on the folded filter, using different colors and shapes (such as rings, dots, or lines). Then let students get started on their own designs, replicating patterns from a real butterfly or making up their own.

The Butterfly Alphabet by Kjell B. Sandved (Scholastic, 1996) features spectacular close-up photos of butterfly wings, each revealing a pattern that resembles a letter in the alphabet, from *A* to *Z*. Facing pages show what the entire butterfly looks like. An annotated glossary in the back of the book gives information about each butterfly featured.

For a creative-writing break, share "How Butterflies Came to Be," from *Keepers of the Animals* by Michael J. Caduto and Joseph Bruchac (Fulcrum, 1991). Then let students work in groups to write their own butterfly stories.

5 When students are finished making their designs, show them how to set the folded tip of the filter in the cup of water. Have students observe what happens. (Thanks to capillary action, the filter soaks up water from the cup; as water reaches the colors, they begin to bleed into one another.)

6 After a few minutes (or when the water has completely soaked the filter), have students remove the filters from the water, open them up, and spread them on newspaper to dry. Ask students to describe how the colors changed. What do they notice about where the patterns appear? (The colors soaked through the folds of the filter, creating mirror-image, repeating patterns all around the circle.)

7 When the filters are dry, hand out clothespins and pipe cleaners. Guide children in following these directions to make their butterflies.

- Pinch the filter together in the middle, then slide it into the clothespin and spread out the wings.

- Insert small pieces of pipe cleaner into the front of the clothespin for antennae. Glue on wiggly eyes (optional).

EXTENSION

Symmetry in Nature: Collect a variety of symmetrical and non-symmetrical objects from nature, such as flowers; rocks; maple seeds; leaves; feathers; shells; mushrooms; and apples, citrus fruits, and onions (sliced in half). Use a pocket mirror to classify the objects as symmetrical or nonsymmetrical. (Place the mirror on the center of an object. If you see the mirror image, the object is symmetrical.) Dip symmetrical objects in paint and use them to make prints.

Critter Hide-and-Seek

Students investigate ways camouflage can help animals survive.

Materials
cardboard
scissors
camouflage materials (such as paint, leaves, grass)
glue
tape

 TIP If possible, plan this activity for a day when students can work outside. It's helpful for students to work on step 3 near the habitats they choose for their critters.

1 Explain to students that they are going to be creating animals that will be hidden in their homes. Take students outside and let them pick places for their critters to live. You might want to limit the area within which students hide their critters. Choose two or three areas and divide the class into groups.

2 Encourage students to look carefully at the colors and shapes around them (for example, green grass, brown leaves, smooth blacktop).

3 Challenge students to create critters that will be camouflaged in this home. Have students consider size and shape, then cut their critters out of cardboard. Using available materials, have students camouflage the critters so they blend into their homes. For example, they might paint them and glue on materials such as leaves or grass, a loose chunk of blacktop, pipe cleaners, cotton, soil, or pebbles to make snakes, bugs, or mice.

4 When students are finished, have them put the critters in their homes then go hunting! How hard or easy is it to find the camouflaged critters? If students spot some critters quickly, encourage them to try to find ways to camouflage them better.

5 In a follow-up discussion, ask: How do you think camouflage helps your critter? (stays safe from predators, can sneak up on prey)

• • • • VARIATION • • • •

TIME FOR A CHANGE: Ask students to consider how their critters' homes might change in winter. How might they need to change the camouflage? Help students research animals such as the snowshoe hare and the ptarmigan that change color with the seasons. (See Book Break, at right.)

 BOOK BREAK

Inspire camouflage investigations with these books.

• *Animal Camouflage, A Closer Look* by Joyce Powzyk (Bradbury Press, 1990). Spot the animals hiding within this book's pages.

• *Hide and Seek* edited by Coldrey and Goldie Morrison (Putnam, 1986). Incredible photographs invite readers into the secret world of animals and camouflage.

• *I See Animals Hiding* by Jim Arnosky (Scholastic, 1995). Soft watercolor paintings and simple text introduce animals that hide by blending into their surroundings and by changing colors with the seasons.

Spiderweb Greeting Cards

Students investigate the structure of spiderwebs by spinning their own.

SCIENCE TALK

Spiders spin their webs using a sticky liquid protein produced in tiny organs in their abdomen. When this liquid comes into contact with air, it hardens into spider silk, a lightweight but extremely strong material. To construct their wheel-shaped webs, orb spiders create an irregular circle of silk, within which they add as many as 50 spokelike threads. Then, working out from the center, they weave a spiral-shaped design, creating a taut but flexible structure. Spiders use their webs as a place to live and to trap insects they eat. From the middle of the web, a spider can sense an insect's presence anywhere on the web.

In this activity, students make their own spiderwebs using string. Although the steps they follow do not model a spider's web-making process exactly, students will develop an appreciation for the intricacy of these woven structures.

Materials
books about spiders (see Book Break, page 35)
12-by-18-inch pieces of colored tagboard, folded in half; or legal-size file folders
    (1 per student)
white string or yarn
scissors
masking tape
pipe cleaners
pompoms
glue

1 Invite students to research different kinds of webs spiders spin. (See Book Break, page 35.)

2 Tell students that they are going to make orb-shaped spiderweb cards. Give each student a piece of folded tagboard and three lengths of string, ranging from 8 to 12 inches. Each will also need another piece of string about 2 yards long. Guide students in making the webs. It will be helpful to make one along with students so that they can see easily what to do in each step.

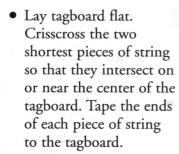

- Lay tagboard flat. Crisscross the two shortest pieces of string so that they intersect on or near the center of the tagboard. Tape the ends of each piece of string to the tagboard.

- Position the third piece of string so it crosses the first two pieces at the center. Wrap this piece around the center of the crossed pieces for strength, then tape each end to the tagboard.

- Use the longer length of string to make the web's spiral shape. Starting near the center, knot a piece of string to one of the taped pieces.

- Move to the next taped piece, knot, and continue the process until the web is complete.

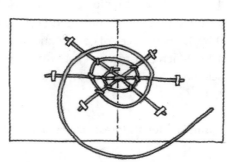

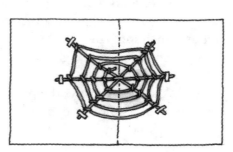

BOOK BREAK

Let students see, step by step, how a garden spider spins its web and uses it to catch food by sharing *Spider's Web* by Christine Back and Barrie Watts (Silver Burdett Press, 1984). Each easy-to-read double-page spread includes a clear diagram of one step in the web-making process. Extraordinary photos of the spider at work fill the opposite pages.

For more eye-popping photos of different kinds of spiders and the webs they weave, share *Amazing Spiders* by Claudia Schnieper (Carolrhoda, 1986) and *Extremely Weird Spiders* by Sarah Lovett (John Muir, 1991).

3 To finish the cards, have students make spiders out of pipe cleaners and pompoms and attach them to their webs. Invite students to think of spider-related messages to write on their cards (for example, "I'm spinning for you," for Valentine's Day). When recipients open their cards, the webs will spread out to create a dramatic 3-D effect.

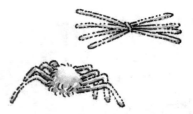

EXTENSION

Web-Finding Walk: Search for spiderwebs outside. Early morning is a good time to spot them as drops of dew on the threads make them more visible. Sketch web designs you see. Return the next day. Have the webs changed?

Nest Test Baskets

Students explore how weaving helps strengthen birds' nests.

Nests give birds a soft, safe place to lay eggs and raise their young. What kinds of materials can protect eggs and baby birds from harm? Twigs, grass, vines, feathers, leaves, and mud are just some of the materials birds use to build their nests. And while many birds weave elaborate basketlike nests, others take a simpler approach. Penguins, for example, make do with a pile of pebbles.

Materials

modeling clay
Nest Test journal page (page 42)
1-by-6-inch construction paper strips (8 strips per group)
1-pound plastic deli containers (1 per group)
9-by-12-inch pieces of construction paper (1 per student)
1-by-9-inch construction paper strips in a contrasting color (9 per student)
scissors
glue
tape
natural materials (grass, leaves, twigs)

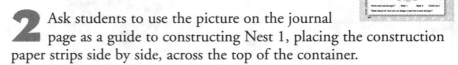

1 Have students work in groups and prepare by making several eggs with the modeling clay, each about 1 inch long and 3/4 inch wide. Give each group a container and eight 1-by-6-inch paper strips.

2 Ask students to use the picture on the journal page as a guide to constructing Nest 1, placing the construction paper strips side by side, across the top of the container.

3 Have students predict and record how many eggs they think Nest 1 will hold before it falls apart.

4 Let students test their predictions, gently placing one egg in the middle of the nest, then adding eggs until the nest collapses. Have students record the number of eggs the nest held before it fell apart.

5 Now have students make Nest 2, this time weaving the eight strips together as shown and repeating steps 3 and 4.

6 Have students share their findings. Which nest held more eggs? (probably Nest 2) Why? (Weaving the strips helps strengthen the paper.)

NEST 1   NEST 2

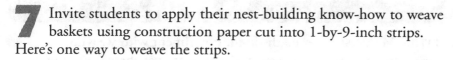

7 Invite students to apply their nest-building know-how to weave baskets using construction paper cut into 1-by-9-inch strips. Here's one way to weave the strips.

- Fold a piece of construction paper in half the short way. Starting at the fold, and 1 inch from one side, cut a straight line through the paper to about 1 inch from the open edge of the paper.

- Repeat this process to make 6 more slits in the paper.

- Open the paper and spread it flat. Weave the first construction paper strip through the slits, weaving over and under them.

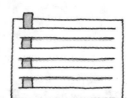

- Continue weaving strips (alternating colors as well) until you have filled the paper. You'll use 8 or 9 strips in all. Push the strips close together as you work. Then glue the edges of the strips in place.

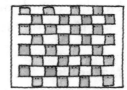

- Fold up two or three strips on each side to create a basket shape. Gently crease the bottom edges of the basket to give them more definition.

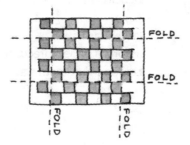

- Pinch each corner and crease. Then fold down the corners and glue them to the sides of the basket.

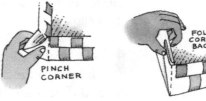

TIP To make baskets more nestlike, let students weave twigs, grass, string, and other materials into their baskets along with the paper strips.

BOOK BREAK

Cradles in the Trees: The Story of Bird Nests by Patricia Brennan Demuth (Macmillan, 1994). Woven nests, mud nests, sewn nests—this book details the variety of nests built by birds with clear watercolor paintings. Includes information about nest location, construction, and materials.

For a fictional account of how birds came to build different kinds of nests, read *The Magpies' Nest* by Joanna Foster (Clarion, 1995). Based on an Old English folktale, this story tells how two magpies give nest-building lessons to other birds. The variety of nests that result show how well their students followed the directions they were given.

PATTERN MAKERS: For a math tie-in, experiment with weaving patterns, for example, over two, under two or over three, under one. Or make wavy-shaped strips and slits instead of straight ones.

WHAT CAN WE WEAVE WITH?: Weave with gift wrap, fabric, or dried grasses and twigs. Gather and display samples of woven products (baskets, different kinds of cloth) for students to examine.

EXTENSION

Nest Detectives: Take a walk to search for birds' nests. If you live where trees lose their leaves in the winter, this is a good time to look for them, because they are easier to spot among bare branches.

Track Tales

Students study animal tracks, then use track-making materials to create note cards, gift wrap, bookmarks, and more.

Materials
Track Trails journal page (page 43)
pencils with erasers
pens
large erasers
assorted paper (precut to size for notecards, gift wrap, and bookmarks)
cardboard or foam trays
scissors
paint
tape
quick-drying clay
assorted objects (forks, crayons, toothpicks, spoons)
paper clips

1 Hand out the Track Trails journal page and ask students to describe what the picture shows. (three different kinds of animal footprints or tracks) Ask: What do you think happened to make these tracks? Expect a lively discussion in which students offer possible scenarios. (Two animals had a skirmish over food; one animal walked into the pond; another animal flew into the pond, and so on.)

2 Summarize by explaining that tracks give us clues about the animal(s) that made them. Ask students what some of these clues might be. (the size, shape, and structures of their feet; what they were doing when they made the tracks; how fast they were moving, and so on)

3 Show students pictures of different kinds of animals and the tracks they make. Then set up stations students can visit to make tracks in different ways. Students may choose to use the materials to show the track pattern of one animal or create scenarios that include several different types. In stations 1 and 2, students can use the materials to make note cards and writing paper, gift wrap, and bookmarks. In station 3, they make track plaques.

Station 1: **Eraser Tracks**

Stock this station with ballpoint pens, different kinds of paper, and assorted erasers (pencil top erasers and large erasers). Post the following directions.

- Use a pen to draw an animal track on an eraser.

- Use the eraser as a rubber stamp to make designs, applying more ink as needed.

Station 2: **Cardboard Cutout Tracks**

Supply cardboard or foam trays, pencils, scissors, tape, paint, and assorted paper. Post these directions.

- Draw a track shape on cardboard. Cut it out. Tape a cardboard tab to one side of the shape.

- Brush paint over the other side of the shape. Press it onto clean paper to make a track.

- Repeat the process to create track patterns.

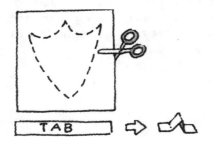

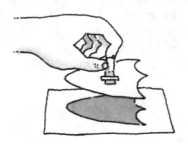

Animal Tracks

Bear

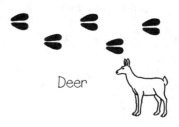

Deer

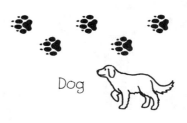

Dog

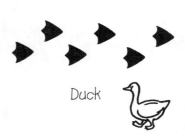

Duck

Raccoon

Station 3: **Track Plaques**

Provide quick-drying clay, assorted objects (such as forks, crayons, toothpicks, spoons), and paper clips. Post these directions.

- Flatten a lump of clay.

- Use different objects to make tracks in the clay (fork or toothpicks to make claws; spoon to make a deep, rounded foot; the end of a crayon or marker to make paw pads).

- Press a paper clip into the clay before it dries to make a hanger for your plaque.

• • • VARIATION • • •

TRACK PATTERN T-SHIRTS: Dip track shapes (cardboard cutouts or potato halves that have tracks cut out in relief) into fabric paint and press onto cotton T-shirts to create different patterns and designs. (Place folded newspaper inside the shirts to prevent paint from leaking through to the back.)

• • • EXTENSION • • •

Stories Tracks Tell: Cut thick cardboard into track shapes, using the pictures on page 39 as reference. Use them to tell track stories, painting or drawing a habitat on butcher paper first, then adding the tracks. Try making tracks that show animals leaping, bounding, waddling, or moving in other ways. Trade track pictures and try to tell the stories with words.

Name _____

Insect Key

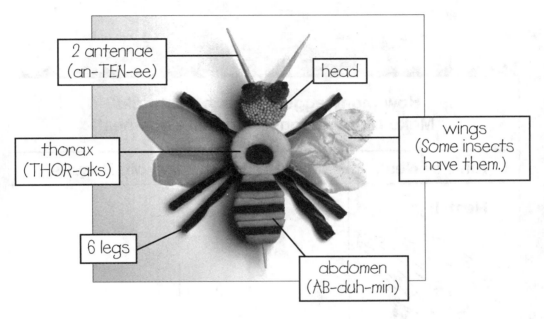

2 antennae
(an-TEN-ee)

head

thorax
(THOR-aks)

wings
(Some insects
have them.)

6 legs

abdomen
(AB-duh-min)

Draw the insect you made.

How is it like the insect in the picture above? How is it different?

_____

_____

_____

Name _____

Nest Test

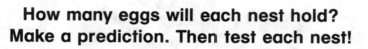

How many eggs will each nest hold?
Make a prediction. Then test each nest!

Kind of Nest	My Prediction	My Results
Nest 1		
Nest 2		

Which nest was stronger?   **Nest 1**   **Nest 2**   (Circle one.)

Think About It: How can you design a nest that is even stronger?

Name _____

Track Trails

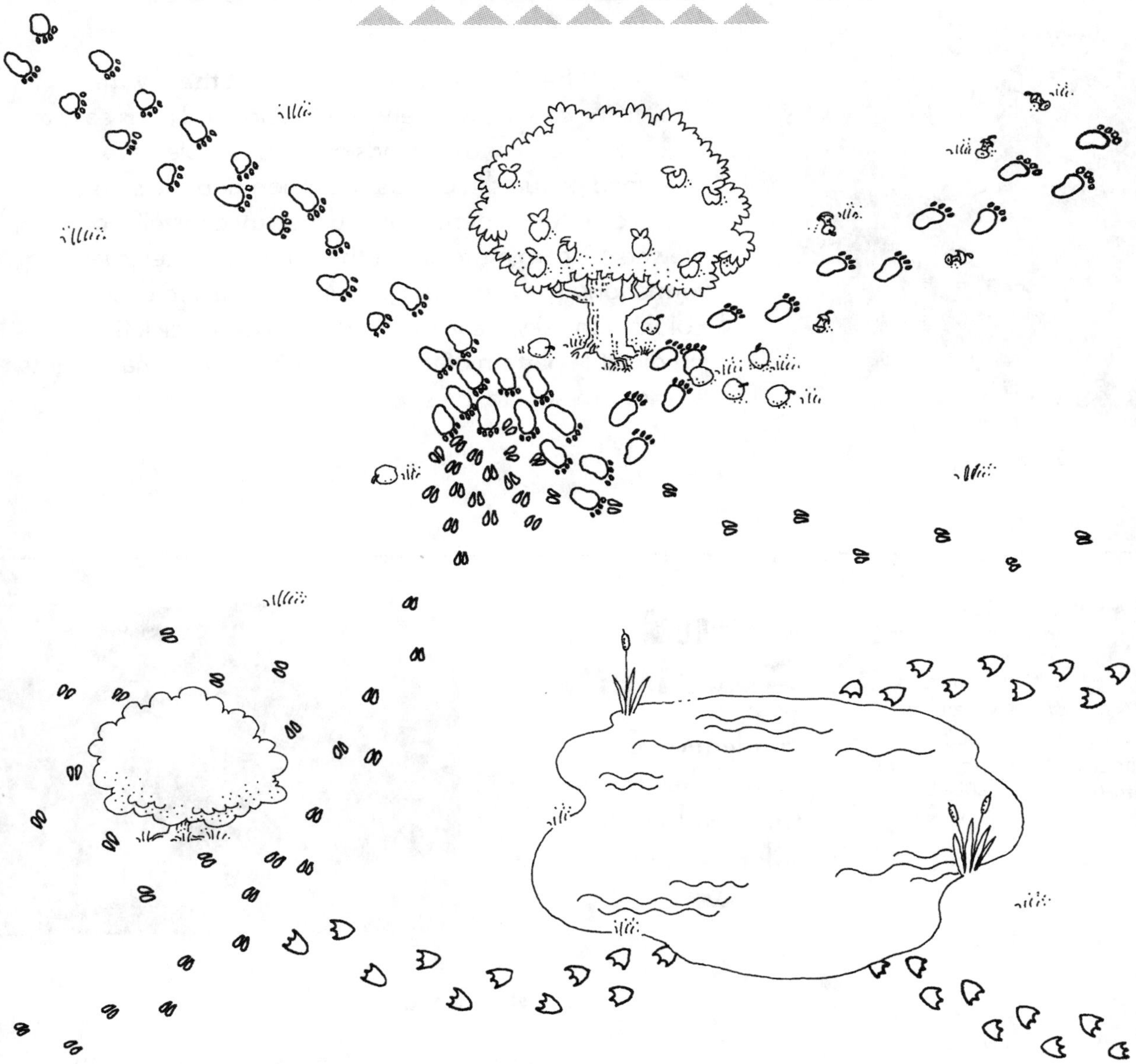

_____
_____
_____
_____
_____
_____

Sky Watch

When it comes to looking up at the sky, the connection between science and art is easy to see. For thousands of years, people have imagined pictures in clouds, the moon, and the stars. In this chapter, students construct starry constellation viewers to learn more about these twinkling celestial formations. They also design cloud catchers to observe colors in the sky, create a sparkly banner to track the predictable pattern of the moon's phases, and make prints as they investigate the sun's power.

Cloud Catchers

Students make viewfinders to help them explore the colors in clouds.

SCIENCE TALK

Clouds form when *water vapor*—water in its gaseous form—condenses on small salt or dust particles suspended in the air. Why do some clouds look white and brighter than others? When cloud droplets are very small, they scatter the sun's light and look very white. But when they combine to form large raindrops, clouds become thicker and block the sun's light. This makes them appear darker. At sunset, clouds take on a variety of different hues. As the sun nears the horizon, its light passes through several layers of Earth's atmosphere. The atmosphere scatters the blue part of sunlight and reflects the reds and oranges, allowing them to pass through. Sunset cloud colors vary depending on the location of the sun in the sky, the humidity, and the type and density of particles in the atmosphere.

Materials

thin cardboard, cut into 9-by-12-inch pieces (1 per student)
scissors
craft sticks or unsharpened pencils (1 per student)
tape
old magazines
glue

1 Guide students in making cloud catchers.

- Fold the cardboard in half.

- Cut a window out of the center, starting at the folded edge.

- Unfold the cardboard and tape a craft stick near one end.

TIP Students might prefer to make their cloud catchers in the shape of a cloud. Instead of a rectangle, have them cut the outside of the folded cardboard into an amorphous cloud shape, then cut out a cloud-shaped window.

2 Invite students to find pictures of clouds in magazines and cut them out. Have them arrange the pictures by cloud color (gray, blue, pink, pinkish-orange, and so on) on their cloud catchers and glue them in place.

3 Take students outside at different times of the day to study clouds in the sky, holding the cloud catchers to their eyes for a focused look. What colors do they see? Have them draw or paint the colors and shapes they see in their science journals.

VARIATIONS

DAWN TO DUSK: Send cloud catchers home for the weekend to observe the sky at sunset. Are the colors the same or different? How about cloud colors at dawn? On fair weather days? Rainy days?

CATCH CLOUD TYPES: Instead of cloud colors, have students research cloud types (cirrus, cumulus, stratus, etc.) and make a cloud catcher using cut-out pictures of these different cloud formations.

Cirrus

Cumulus

Cumulonimbus

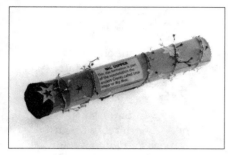

Starry Constellation Viewers

Students create constellations to learn about the familiar patterns of stars in the sky.

Stars are hot balls of gas and dust that radiate heat and light and appear in the night sky as small points of light. Since ancient times, different people and cultures have grouped stars into recognizable patterns called *constellations.* Modern sky charts divide the sky into 88 constellations. Though the stars in each constellation appear to be close together, they are actually many light-years apart. Star distances are measured in light-years. Light travels at about 186,000 miles per second. In one year, light would travel about 6 trillion miles, or one light-year.

The Big Dipper

Materials

newspapers
Starry Constellations pattern page (page 51)
scissors
black construction paper, cut into 3-inch squares (1 per student)
straight pins (1 per student)
paper towel or bathroom tissue tubes (1 per student)
rubber bands or tape
assorted art supplies such as star-shaped stickers, neon paint, glitter
flashlight (optional)

SAFETY NOTE

Caution students to be careful when they use the pins to make their constellation patterns.

1 Hand out the Starry Constellations pattern page. Read and discuss the constellation cards. Then guide students to make their starry constellation viewers.

- Cover a work space with several layers of folded newspaper.

- Choose a constellation from the pattern page and cut it out along the dotted line. Cut out its constellation card too.

- Place the black construction paper on top of the newspaper. Then place the constellation you want to make on top of the black paper.

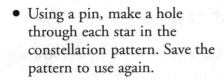 

- Using a pin, make a hole through each star in the constellation pattern. Save the pattern to use again.

- Center the black paper over one end of the tube so the star pattern is within the opening.

- Fold the paper around the tube and use a rubber band or tape to hold it in place. Trim off excess paper.

- Tape the constellation card on the tube. Decorate your tube with neon paint (it glows in the dark!), star-shaped stickers, and glitter.

2 To view their constellations, have students hold the tubes toward a light and look through the open end. For a more dramatic effect, dim the lights and let students take turns pointing their tubes toward a wall and shining a flashlight through the open end. Constellations will appear on the wall.

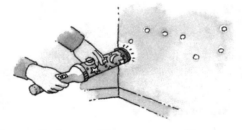

● ● ● V A R I A T I O N S ● ● ●

STARRY SKY BOOKMARKS: On black construction paper strips (about 2 by 8 inches each), make dots with a pencil or a white crayon to represent stars in constellations. Place a small dot of glue over each dot and sprinkle with glitter. Tap off excess and let dry.

3-D CONSTELLATIONS: Construct three-dimensional models of different constellations using mini-marshmallows and toothpicks. Can students guess the names of the constellations their classmates make?

● ● ● E X T E N S I O N ● ● ●

Home-School Connection: Encourage students to go stargazing with their families. How many constellations can they identify in the night sky? If possible, let students take turns borrowing a guide to the night sky, such as *The Glow-in-the-Dark Night Sky Book* by Clint Hatchett (Random House, 1988).

BOOK BREAK

Invite students to learn more about the night sky with these books.

- *Star Tales* and *More Star Tales* by Gretchen Will Mayo (Walker, 1987). Learn about the white river in the sky (the Milky Way), birds of summer (the Big Dipper), and dancing braves (the Pleiades) with this collection of Native American stories.

- *Night Sky: How to Observe and Understand the Mysteries of the Night Sky*, an Eyewitness Explorers book by Carole Stott (Dorling Kindersley, 1993). This pocket-sized practical guide is filled with stories, projects, and fun facts.

- *The Night of the Stars* by Douglas Gutierrez and Maria Fernandez Oliver (Kane/Miller Books, 1988). Learn what happens when a man who despises darkness climbs to the top of the highest mountain and pokes holes in the sky.

Picture the Moon

Students discover the predictable pattern of the moon's phases as they create a sparkly moon banner.

SCIENCE TALK

The moon rotates on its axis at the same speed as it revolves around Earth. (The time from one full moon to the next is 29 1/2 days.) As a result, we always see the same side of the moon. Since the moon circles Earth, different parts of this side get illuminated by the sun depending on where the moon is in its orbit. The reflected shapes we see are called *phases* (from the Greek word *phaino*, meaning "to bring light"). The rest of the moon seems to have disappeared because it is not being lit by the sun. While these concepts are difficult for young children to grasp, this activity lets them observe how the moon seems to change and builds a foundation for future explorations and understanding.

New · Waxing crescent · First quarter · Waxing gibbous · Full · Waning gibbous · Last quarter · Waning crescent

Materials

drawing paper
crayons
calandar or almanac
roll of bulletin board paper
white crayons
black watercolor or thinned tempera paint
paintbrushes
newspaper
salt

1 Ask students to draw a picture of the moon. Then invite them to share their drawings. Do all of the moons look the same? (Some students may draw full moons, others may draw crescents.) Ask: Does the moon look the same each night during the month? Invite students to share what they know or have observed.

TIP Try to start this activity around the time of the new moon. Check a calendar or an almanac for the date. These resources will also come in handy for times when the moon is not visible or when moonrise takes place when students are asleep.

2 Assign each student one night to look for the moon, record how it looks on a piece of paper, and bring that paper to school the next day. (You might assign two students per night in the event of absences or forgetfulness.)

3 Place a roll of bulletin board paper on the floor. Each day, ask the child who recorded the moon the previous night to draw the moon's shape on the paper, using white crayon and filling in the shape completely. Be sure students add their moon shapes in order.

4 Repeat this process throughout the month (or until the next new moon, a cycle of about 29 days). Cut the banner from the roll of paper and place on newspaper.

5 Invite students to paint over and around their moon shapes with black paint. The moon shapes will emerge from the painted background because of the waxy crayons' resistance to the water-based paint. For a sparkly effect, sprinkle salt over the banner while the paint is still wet. Let dry.

6 Ask students to describe how the moon changed. Challenge them to predict how the moon might look on the following night.

EXTENSION

Moon Phases and Names: Learn the names of the moon phases (new, crescent, quarter, gibbous) and label them on the banner. *Where Does the Moon Go?* by Sidney Roden (Carolrhoda, 1992) is a good book to use for reference.

BOOK BREAK

Have students ever heard of the harvest moon? The September moon's name came from the full moon, which gives farmers extra light for harvesting crops. The moons in other months have special names, too, such as January's wolf moon (when winter's bite is at its worst) and April's pink moon (when the first flowers of spring appear). Explore other moon names with *Twelve Moons* (G.K. Hall, 1985), a collection of nature essays by Hal Borland. Follow up by inviting students to come up with their own moon names, based on seasonal weather and events in their area.

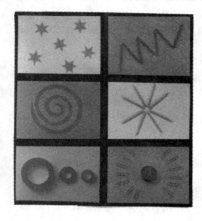

Sun Power Prints

Students explore the power of the sun, our nearest star, to make a sun print quilt.

The sun is about 93 million miles away from Earth. Yet its powerful energy makes life possible on our planet. In this activity, when construction paper is exposed to strong sunlight, the dyes in the paper undergo a chemical change, breaking down and causing the paper to fade. Areas covered by objects are protected from sunlight and keep their color.

Materials

printmaking objects (such as leaves, keys, feathers, shapes cut out of construction paper)

dark colors of construction paper (1 piece per student)

masking tape or colored tape

1 Invite each student to choose several objects to make a sun print. Guide students in following these steps.

- Place a piece of dark construction paper on a sunny windowsill.

- Set your objects on the paper. (Make another setup in a spot away from the sun to compare results.)

- The next day, lift up one of your objects. What changes do you see on the paper? (The paper surrounding the object has faded.)

- Every day, lift up another object.

2 When students have lifted up all of their objects, ask: Can you tell where an object stayed on longer? What happened to the setup in the shade? (no changes)

3 Have students carefully replace their objects on the papers (tape lightweight objects in place). Leave the objects in place for about a week (two if you have intermittent sunshine).

4 After a week, have students remove the objects, then work together to arrange their prints to make a quilt. Line up the edges of the papers and tape together (or glue to bulletin board paper), then display. Can students match objects with prints?

SAFETY NOTE

Remind students not to look directly at the sun, as this can harm their eyes.

BOOK BREAK

The Sun by Seymour Simon (William Morrow, 1986) contains stunning photos and fascinating facts about the sun, our nearest star.

Explore more sky phenomena such as shooting meteors, clouds, the moon, and the stars with *Sky Worlds* (Macmillan, 1994), a collection of poems by Marilyn Singer. Let interested students copy favorite poems on construction paper cut in sky shapes and create a display.

Starry Constellations

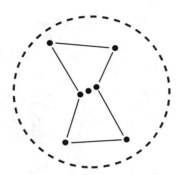

Orion
Orion was a famous hunter in Greek mythology. Three bright stars across his middle make his belt.

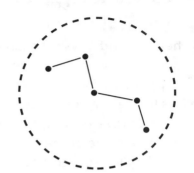

Cassiopeia
To the ancient Greeks, this group of stars looked like Cassiopeia, a powerful queen sitting on her throne.

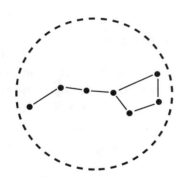

Big Dipper
These stars look like a giant ice cream scoop. The Big Dipper is part of a larger constellation called the Great Bear.

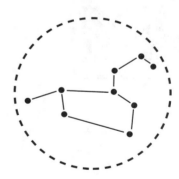

Leo
Leo means "lion." This star group looked like a lion to the ancient Greeks. Does it look like a lion to you?

ScienceART   Scholastic Professional Books

Changes

Chemical and physical changes are part of our everyday lives—from what happens when a cake bakes or sugar caramelizes to the way toothpaste foams on our teeth or ice melts in a glass. In this chapter, students explore some of these changes for themselves. They'll discover that some changes happen quickly—as when they use chemical reactions to create color-changing chameleons. Other changes take place more slowly—as when they make saturated solutions to create sparkly crystals or dry apples to make puppet faces.

Send a Secret Message!

Students explore chemical changes when they make greeting cards with invisible ink.

SCIENCE TALK

Fruit juices, milk, and sugar contain carbon compounds. Heat causes these compounds to break down and turn brown or black. The same process caramelizes sugar, makes marshmallows dark and crispy, and turns bread into brown toast.

Materials (for each group)

lemon or grapefruit juice
milk
cotton swabs
small paper cups
8 1/2-by-11-inch white paper and construction paper
scissors
glue
lamp or iron
paper grocery bag
decorating materials such as markers, paper scraps, glitter

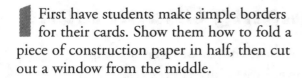

1 First have students make simple borders for their cards. Show them how to fold a piece of construction paper in half, then cut out a window from the middle.

 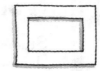

2 Have students glue the border on top of the white paper, being careful to line up the edges.

3 Give each small group of students cups filled with lemon or grapefruit juice, milk, and cotton swabs.

4 Tell students to dip a cotton swab into one of the liquids and use it to write a message to a friend on the paper inside the frame.

5 While the messages dry, let students decorate the borders of their cards. As they work, ask students to observe what happens to the liquids. (They become invisible as they dry.)

6 Have students swap cards, then take turns lightly rubbing the white paper over a warm lightbulb, being careful not to touch the lightbulb. What happens? (The message reappears in brown or black.) Ask students to explain why they think this happened. (Heat caused a chemical reaction to take place.)

 TIP For faster results, sandwich students' papers between a folded paper grocery bag and rub with a medium-hot iron.

• • • • VARIATION • • • •

SEND A LOVE NOTE: To make Valentine's Day cards, combine this activity with What Is Red? (page 71). Have students use an assortment of shades of red paper to cover their frames and write secret valentine messages inside the frames.

• • • EXTENSION • • •

More Invisible Inks: Try using other kinds of juices or a teaspoon of baking powder or confectioner's sugar mixed with a little water to make invisible inks and compare results.

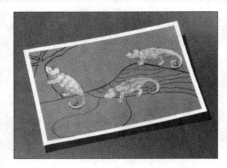

Color-Changing Chameleons

Students use an acid and base indicator to create paper chameleons that change colors before their eyes!

SCIENCE TALK

Grape juice contains a chemical that changes color based on a substance's acidity or pH. When grape juice comes into contact with baking soda (a base), as in this activity, it turns bluish-green. With vinegar, grape juice turns pinkish-red. If a substance is neither an acid nor a base, it is neutral and no color change occurs. The concept of acids and bases is too abstract for young students to understand. Use this activity to help students begin to recognize that chemical reactions cause changes to take place. This will lay the foundation for a more detailed understanding of chemistry concepts later on.

BOOK BREAK

Students will love the amazing photos of real chameleons changing color in *Chameleons: Dragons in the Trees* by James Martin (Crown, 1991). And they'll be spellbound by the stop-action photos showing a chameleon snap a bug with its long, sticky tongue!

Materials (for each group)

Color-Changing Chameleons pattern page (page 68)
scissors
purple grape juice
paper cups
cotton swabs
paper towels
measuring spoons
baking soda
water
vinegar
smocks

1 Hand out the pattern page and have students cut out the chameleons.

2 Divide students into groups, giving each a cup of grape juice and a handful of cotton swabs. Have students place a chameleon on a paper towel, then use a cotton swab to paint it completely with grape juice. Let the chameleons dry several hours or overnight.

3 Then prepare the following for each group: In one cup, dissolve 1 tablespoon baking soda in 3 tablespoons water. Pour vinegar in the second cup. Label both cups.

4 Ask students to dip cotton swabs in the baking soda cup and dab the painted chameleon's tail. What happens? (The spot turns bluish-green.)

5 Have them dip fresh cotton swabs in the vinegar and dab another spot on the chameleon. What happens this time? (The spot turns pink.) Ask students to explain why they think it's important to use a fresh cotton swab each time they paint with a different substance. (to avoid contaminating the liquids)

6 Invite students to explain why they think the chameleons changed colors. (A chemical reaction took place.)
Ask: Can you think of a way to make the dots disappear? Invite them to try their ideas. (Dab the vinegar spot with baking soda; dab the baking soda spot with vinegar.)

7 Let students use the acid and base paints to make their other chameleons change color.

SAFETY NOTE

To avoid stinging their eyes, tell students to keep their fingers out of their eyes and to wash their hands after painting with the vinegar. If vinegar does get into a child's eyes, rinse with cool water.

VARIATIONS

CHANGE OF PLANS: What happens if you paint first with the baking soda or vinegar, then brush on the grape juice later? Investigate and find out.

CRANBERRY COLORS: For a fun project at Thanksgiving time, repeat the activity using cranberries instead of grape juice as an indicator. Simply squeeze a berry and rub its juice over the paper.

WHAT ELSE CHANGES COLOR?: Bring in other substances such as apple and lemon juice, coffee, egg whites, milk, sugar water, salt water, tea, milk, dishwashing liquid, and carbonated soda. Predict which will cause color changes (and how), then work in teams to test them. Let teams share their findings. Chart results.

Crystal Chemistry

In this next set of related activities, students explore the amazing world of crystals. As they make beautiful decorations, they'll learn about the properties of matter and physical change.

SCIENCE TALK

Salt, sugar, and Epsom salts are all examples of crystals—solids with flat sides and a symmetrical shape because their molecules are arranged in a unique, repeating pattern. All crystals of the same type have the same internal structure. That's why Epsom salts crystals may be large or small but are all needle-shaped, and salt crystals are always cube-shaped.

How do the Epsom salts crystals grow? Hot water holds more Epsom salts crystals than cold water does. That's because heated water molecules move farther apart, making room for more of the Epsom salts crystals to dissolve. When no more of the crystals can be dissolved, you have a saturated solution. As this solution cools, the water molecules move closer together again. Now there's less room for the solution to hold onto as much of the dissolved salts. Crystals begin to form and build on one another as the water lets go of the excess and evaporates.

Part 1: Close-up on Crystals

Materials (for each group)
salt
Epsom salts
sugar
small paper cups
glue stick or tape
Close-up on Crystals journal page (page 69)
hand lenses

1 Put a few tablespoons each of salt, Epsom salts, and sugar into separate paper cups. Label the cups. You'll need a set of cups for each group.

2 Ask students to use the glue stick to make nickel-sized dots on the black squares on their journal pages. Then have them sprinkle a few grains of each substance on the squares.

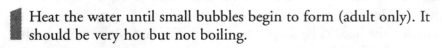

TIP If you use tape instead of the glue stick, have students first sprinkle the crystals on the black squares, then cover them with tape.

3 Have students use the hand lenses to examine the crystals. What differences and similarities do they observe? (shape, size) Have students draw and describe the shape of each crystal on their science journal pages. Explain that the salt, Epsom salts, and sugar particles start out larger than these samples. But they have been broken down during manufacturing and packaging.

Part 2: Crystal Creations

Students see a solution change into sparkling crystals they can hang in a window.

Materials
stove or hot plate
saucepan
3 cups water
4 cups Epsom salts
wooden spoon
several large, clear wide-mouth glass jars
    (pickle or spaghetti sauce jars work well)
ruler
pipe cleaners
thin string or thread
craft sticks
tape
large, clear plastic cups (1 per student)
paper towels
food coloring (optional)
hand lenses

1 Heat the water until small bubbles begin to form (adult only). It should be very hot but not boiling.

2 Slowly stir the Epsom salts into the hot water, one spoonful at a time. Let students take turns looking in the pan. Ask: What's happening to the Epsom salts crystals? (Students may think that the Epsom salts disappear when they dissolve.) Pour the solution into the glass jars and let it cool.

TIP To help students understand that the salts are still in the water even after they've dissolved, use a clean ruler to measure the water level in the pan before and after adding the Epsom salts. Then have students observe the difference in measurements.

SAFETY NOTE

 Have students wash their hands after handling the Epsom salts solution in this activity.

3 Meanwhile, have students prepare decorative shapes for dipping in the Epsom salts solution.

- Bend a pipe cleaner into a simple shape such as a half moon, heart, or spiral. The shape must be small enough to fit inside a plastic cup. (Or you can use larger cups or containers from cottage cheese or yogurt.)

- Tie one end of an 8-inch piece of string or thread to the shape. Tape the other end to a craft stick.

4 Pour the cooled Epsom salts solution into the plastic cups. For colorful crystals, students can add a few drops of food coloring to the cups. Have students dip their shapes in the solution, laying the craft stick across the top of the cup, checking that their shape does not touch the sides or bottom of the cup. Set the cups in a place where they won't be disturbed overnight. Ask students to predict what they will see the next day.

5 The following day, have students gently pull their shapes out of the cup and place them on a paper towel to dry. What changes do they see? (The dissolved Epsom salts have turned into long, thick, needlelike crystals.)

6 Invite students to use hand lenses to compare their crystal creations with the shape and size of the Epsom salts crystals on their science journal pages and record observations in their science journals. (Students may detect some similarities in shape between the crystals. However, since packaged Epsom salts are ground into smaller particles, the needlelike shape may not be obvious.) Ask students what they think might happen if they left the shapes in the crystal solution longer. Invite them to test their ideas. (The crystals continue to grow and get larger.) For another investigation, ask students why they dissolved the Epsom salts in hot water instead of cold.

 TIP Tap water may contain minerals that interfere with the crystal-growing process. If you have trouble growing crystals, try using distilled water instead.

58

SHAPE-CHANGING CRYSTALS: For jewel-like octagon-shaped crystals, use alum powder (available at pharmacies) instead of Epsom salts. Use about 1 1/2 cups of alum for every 4 cups of water. Or try using solutions of salt and water to make cube-shaped crystals or sugar and water to grow chunky-shaped rock candy crystals.

SPARKLING SNOWFLAKES: Make paper snowflakes using black construction paper or transparent, colored plastic sheets (report covers work well). Pour the cooled Epsom salts solution into a glass baking dish. (To help the solution adhere better to the plastic, add a drop of dishwashing liquid.) Dip snowflakes in the dish, then lay on a paper towel to dry.

CRYSTAL JEWELRY: Grow crystals on a piece of string to make a bracelet or necklace. Or glue crystals to a jewelry pin back to make a sparkly brooch.

PAINTING WITH CRYSTALS: Draw a picture with black crayon on dark construction paper. Use a paintbrush or cotton swab to brush the Epsom salts solution over the design and let it dry.

Apple Face Puppets

Students explore evaporation by drying apples to make puppets that are perfect for Halloween.

As the apples in this activity dry, they turn brown due to *oxidation* (a chemical change) and shrivel because of water loss or *evaporation* (a physical change). Evaporation, the process by which water in its liquid state changes to water vapor, occurs when water molecules inside the apples heat up, causing them to move faster and farther apart. When this happens, the water molecules escape into the air as water vapor.

What keeps the apples from rotting? Removing the skin helps water evaporate from them faster. Without water, bacteria and mold cannot grow. To demonstrate this, seal an apple slice in a plastic bag and observe the mold that appears after a few days.

Materials

peeled apples (1 per student)
craft sticks (1 per student)
plastic knives
small beads, uncooked rice, whole cloves, seeds, toothpicks
nonhardening clay
tall cup or container (1 per student)
Apple Faces journal page (page 70)
cheesecloth
pipe cleaners
decorating materials such as lightweight fabric, tissue paper, yarn, old socks
scissors

TIP Though removing the apple skin helps water evaporate and prevent mold, a small amount of mold may still develop as the apples dry. To prevent this, soak the carved apples in a saltwater solution overnight before letting them dry in the cups. (The salt water kills bacteria.) Mix 1/4 cup of salt to every 4 cups of water. Fill the container completely and cover to keep the apples submerged.

1 Give each student an apple and a craft stick. Guide them to prepare their apple face puppets.

- Push the craft stick about halfway into the bottom of the apple.

- Use a plastic knife to carve features on the face, such as a nose, mouth, and so on. Use beads, rice, or other small items for eyes and other details.

- Place a bit of clay in the bottom of a cup and push the end of the craft stick into it, making sure the apple doesn't touch the side of the cup. If the craft stick won't stand up straight, stuff the cup with crumpled newspaper and insert the craft stick into the middle.

2 Ask students to fill in their Apple Faces charts and draw pictures of their apple faces. Also ask them to predict how the apples might change. To protect the apples from dust and bugs, loosely wrap squares of cheesecloth around them. Set the apples, in their cups, in a warm, dry place.

TIP To provide evidence of water loss, have students weigh their apples before and after drying.

3 Have students check their apples regularly for two weeks and observe changes. As the apples dry, students can squeeze them to mold different features on their faces, such as long noses or pointy chins. After two weeks, have students record their observations on the charts. Ask them to compare observations of their apples before and after drying. Encourage them to use descriptive words.

4 Invite students to create and decorate puppets. Here are two ways.

- Wrap a pipe cleaner around the craft stick and bend each end to become the puppet's arms. Then poke the craft stick through a piece of fabric, snip two armholes, and pull the arms through. Add extra pipe cleaners to form other features, such as a waist or legs. Glue on yarn for hair, and fabric scraps, sequins, or other decorations.

- Use an old sock for the puppet's body. Cut a small hole in the toe and a hole on each side. Decorate as suggested above. To manipulate the puppet, poke your fingers through the holes.

E X T E N S I O N

Patterned Pomander Balls: People long ago used pomander balls as natural deodorizers.

- Use a nail to make tiny holes in the skin of an orange or lemon.

- Make a pattern such as a star or a circle, or create a repeating pattern such as stripes. Make extra holes too.

- Push the pointed ends of whole cloves into the pattern holes. Leave the extra holes empty.

- Sprinkle spices such as cinnamon, allspice, and nutmeg into a plastic bag, add the fruit, and shake to cover it with the spices.

- Crisscross a ribbon around the fruit, tie at the top, and hang up the fruit ball for a few weeks. Over time, as water evaporates from the fruit, it will get smaller and harder, creating a sweet-smelling decoration that's great for gift giving.

Dry & Nibble Necklaces

Students investigate how drying changes foods, making this a great activity to plan for harvest and Thanksgiving themes.

Materials

seeds from a pumpkin
raisins
fresh or frozen corn kernels
paper cups
button thread or unwaxed dental floss
scissors
needles with large eyes
cookie sheets
aluminum foil
oven
paper towels
measuring stick

1 Hand out cups of pumpkin seeds, raisins, and corn for groups of students to share. Invite students to taste each of the foods.

2 Show students how to thread a needle (using about 2 1/2 feet of thread) and then use it to string the foods, creating patterns if they like. Have students leave a few inches unstrung at both ends to knot the necklace.

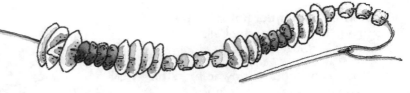

3 Cover cookie sheets with foil and spread students' necklaces on them. Use the dull side of a needle to write students' initials inside their necklaces. Place the cookie sheets in a 250°F oven. Heat until the necklaces have dried, about one hour.

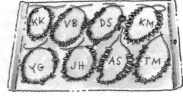

4 Place necklaces on paper towels. As they cool, have students discuss and record in their science journals how heat from the oven changed each of the foods. (See Science Talk, page 59 for information about evaporation.) Invite students to tie the necklaces around their necks and take a nibble when they get hungry. How does drying change the taste of each food?

May Day Paper Baskets

Students investigate how substances change, then use what they learn to build springtime baskets.

SCIENCE TALK

The flour-and-water paste used in papier-mâché is sticky when wet. But, like other adhesives, it strengthens and hardens as it dries.

Materials
newspapers
waxed paper
flour
water
craft sticks
newspaper, comics, and colored tissue paper
plastic bowls or containers (1 per group, plus 1 per student)
balloons (1 per student)
spoon
yarn
scissors
smocks

TIP Check with the cafeteria to see if they have bowls you can borrow. Though they will get messy, they'll clean up with soap and water. Plastic disposable bowls or large containers from cottage cheese or yogurt work fine, too. (You can rinse and save these for other projects.)

1 Set up work areas for groups of students, covering each with newspaper. Begin by asking them to name things that are sticky. (glue, jam, honey, tape) Ask: Is flour sticky? How about water?

2 Give each student a piece of waxed paper about 6 to 8 inches long. Put about a teaspoon of flour on one side of the paper. Put a few drops of water opposite the flour. Have students compare the properties of each, recording observations in their science journals.

3 Hand out craft sticks. Have students use them to mix the flour and water together. Ask students to describe how the two substances change when they are combined and record this in their journals. (The flour and water make a thick, sticky liquid.)

4 Distribute flour, water, newspaper, comics, tissue paper, and bowls to each group, as well as one balloon per student. Have groups prepare their materials, mixing equal parts of flour and water until smooth, tearing newspaper and tissue paper into strips, cutting yarn into yard-long pieces (one piece each), and blowing up and tying their balloons.

5 Demonstrate how to apply strips to the balloons to make a basket.

- Set the balloon upside down in a bowl. This will keep it steady. Dip a paper strip into the paste, lay the strip on the bottom of the balloon, then smooth it out.

- Continue adding strips and paste, making sure they overlap. Cover only the bottom half of the balloon. Build up three or four layers of strips.

- Optional: For the final layer, use overlapping strips of tissue paper instead of newspaper. This gives the basket a colorful effect.

- Make a rim and handle by dipping a piece of yarn into the paste and squeezing off any excess. Wrap around the balloon as shown.

TIP Strips about 1 by 6 inches work well. If the paste thickens as students work, add a little more water. For a faster cleanup, wipe up excess paste while still wet.

6 For even drying, hang the balloons where air can circulate around them. For example, tie the knotted ends to a length of string stretched across a corner of your classroom.

7 The following day, have students pop the balloons and pull them out of the baskets. Ask: How did the paste change after it dried? What would happen to your basket if you used water without flour?

· · · V A R I A T I O N S · · ·

STRING BASKETS AND ORNAMENTS: Instead of using newspaper strips, dip string or yarn in the paste, then wrap it around the balloon, overlapping as you go. To make an ornament with an airy, open design, leave larger spaces between the string as you wrap it around the balloon.

HATS ON! Take two large circles or squares of wrapping paper and apply flour-and-water paste to the plain side of one piece. Place the other piece on top, with the pattern side facing out. Put the paper on your head (pattern side out) and squash it down so the paper takes the shape of your head. Carefully lift off the hat and let it dry. Add ribbons, feathers, beads, tissue paper flowers, or other decorations.

Sand Castle Construction

Students investigate how adhesives can strengthen sand structures.

SCIENCE TALK

Sand is a granular solid. Each grain has its own definite shape. But a pile of sand behaves like a liquid. It can be poured and takes the shape of the container holding it. Sand castles hold their shape because water helps the sand *cohere* or stick together. As the water evaporates, however, the castles turn into sand piles or fall apart when touched. When glue or another adhesive substance is added to the sand, it bonds to the sand grains, making them stick together to form a hard structure.

Materials

small plastic trays (foam meat trays work well) (1 per student)
small paper cups
sand
hand lenses
teaspoon
water
adhesive materials (glue, salt water)
decorating materials (shells, colored toothpicks, beads, paper scraps)

1 Give each student a small plastic tray and a paper cup with about 1/2 cup sand. Have students use hand lenses to observe the sand's properties (color, size, shape) and record observations in their journals.

 If sand isn't readily available, check lumber, hardware, or plant stores. Make sure you use play sand, which has been filtered and washed.

2 Have students add about 2 teaspoons of water to their sand, mix, then use the sand mixture to make sand castles on their trays. When they're finished, have students place their trays in a place where they won't be disturbed overnight.

Because sand textures vary, students may need to adjust the amount of water they add when they make their castles. The sand should be damp but not too wet, or it won't hold together. To shape their castles, students can use their fingers, plastic utensils, or molds such as small paper cups, plastic eggs, cardboard cones, etc.

3 The next day, have students check their castles. Ask: What happens when you touch them? Do the castles hold together or fall apart? (fall apart)

4 Ask students how they might make a sand castle last. Add something to the sand? Make a cover for the castle? Have students record their ideas in their science journals then choose an idea to test. (Sand mixed with school glue and water makes a hard sand castle. Saltwater and sugar water solutions make effective short-term adhesives. Another option is to slow evaporation by placing a plastic cup over the sand castle, then sealing it to the tray so no air can get in.) Have extra sand on hand for students who want to try several ideas.

5 Again, have students put their trays away overnight. The following day, let them touch their castles. Discuss which solutions were most successful.

6 Have students use their most effective solutions to make sand castle paperweights.

• Before the sand castles dry, write a greeting on a flag-shaped piece of paper, glue to a colored toothpick, and stick it into the castle.

• When the castle dries, decorate it by gluing on sequins, small buttons, or other objects. A sand castle paperweight makes a great gift!

⋅ ⋅ ⋅ ⋅ VARIATION ⋅ ⋅ ⋅ ⋅

To make a sand castle note holder, curl the end of a pipe cleaner into a spiral shape and stick it into the sand castle. When it dries, slip removable notes (reminders, questions, greetings) into the coils of the spiral.

Color-Changing Chameleons

Name _____

Close-up on Crystals

Glue or tape a sample of each crystal in the boxes below.

Draw how the crystals look in the boxes below.

Salt

Sugar

Epsom salts

Name _____

Apple Faces

Describe your apple before and after drying.

	Fresh Apple	Dried Apple
Looks		
Feels		
Smells		

Draw a picture of your apple face.

Think About It: How is your dried apple different from a fresh one?

Light, Color & Shadow

Where do colors come from? What makes a rainbow? Why do we see shadows? The projects here invite students to discover answers to these and other questions as they create colorful collages and kaleidoscopes, experiment with mixing colors, paint like the great pointillist Georges Seurat, make shadow portraits, and more!

What Is Red?

Students explore and classify the many shades of red to create colorful collages, perfect for Valentine's Day fun.

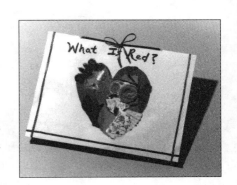

▲▲▲▲▲▲▲▲▲▲▲▲▲▲▲▲▲▲▲▲▲▲▲▲▲▲▲▲▲▲▲▲▲▲
SCIENCE TALK

Why do we see different shades of red? White light from the sun is made up of all the colors of the rainbow, also known as the spectrum. When white light hits a piece of red paper, for example, the pigments in the paper reflect the red in the light and absorb the rest of the colors, so we see red. We see different shades of red when the paper reflects small amounts of other colors.

Materials
old magazines, wallpaper sample books, paint color cards, clothing catalogs, used gift wrap, colored tissue paper

scissors

construction paper

glue or paste

red paint, markers, crayons

1 Read the poem "What Is Pink?" below. Before you start, invite children to answer the question in the poem's title. After reading, ask students to add their own ideas for things that are red. (watermelon, cardinals, some tulips, fire trucks, stop signs) List suggestions on the board, then ask: Is the color red always the same color? Have students compare the particular colors of each item on the list.

What Is Pink?

What is pink? a rose is pink
By the fountain's brink.
What is red? a poppy's red
In its barley bed.
What is blue? the sky is blue
Where the clouds float thro'.
What is white? a swan is white
Sailing in the light.
What is yellow? pears are yellow,
Rich and ripe and mellow.
What is green? the grass is green,
With small flowers between.
What is violet? clouds are violet
In the summer twilight.
What is orange? why, an orange,
Just an orange!

—*Christina G. Rossetti*

BOOK BREAK

Inspire the poets in your students with *Hailstones and Halibut Bones* by Mary O'Neill (Doubleday, 1989), a poetic tribute to different colors that will delight and set the stage for students to write poems about their favorite colors.

2 Challenge students to find examples of the color red from different sources (pictures in old magazines, paint color cards from paint stores, used gift wrap, wallpaper sample books, clothing catalogs).

3 Have students spread out their color samples on their desks. Ask: How are the reds the same? How are they different? Have students group the samples by varying shades (magenta, cherry, burgundy, red-orange, pinkish-red, and so on). To develop vocabulary, encourage students to research the names of other red shades such as crimson, ruby, salmon, scarlet, vermilion, maroon, etc.

4 Invite students to use their color samples to create Valentine's Day cards. Have them rip or cut their color samples into different shapes, then arrange the pieces to make heart-shaped collages on sheets of construction paper folded in half. To fill in spaces, or enhance their designs, students can add different shades of red using paint, markers, or crayons as well as red objects.

TIP Before pasting their paper in place, have students experiment with arranging lighter shades toward the center of the design and darker shades around the edges, or vice versa.

5 Invite students to write their own What Is Red? poems inside their cards.

V A R I A T I O N

WHAT IS GREEN? Repeat the activity with other colors for different celebrations. On Earth Day, for example, have students search for examples of the color green. Don't limit your search to items indoors—go outside for a green scavenger hunt. Invite students to make tree-shaped collages using the different shades of green they find.

BOOK BREAK

How are worms responsible for the color word *crimson*? Students will find out in *Naming Colors* by Adrienne Dewey (HarperCollins, 1995). This fascinating book explores how different colors got their names and where different pigments come from. This book is also great to pull out when you do the Painting with Plants activity (see page 22). By the way, crimson derives from the Sanskrit word *krimi-s* meaning "worm." People long ago extracted rich red dyes from the heart-shaped kermes worm.

Rainbow Light Catchers

Students mix colors to make aquatic creatures in the colors of the rainbow.

SCIENCE TALK

A rainbow forms when white light from the sun shines through water droplets. The droplets *refract* or bend the light, breaking it up into the different colors of the spectrum—red, orange, yellow, green, blue, and violet. An easy way for students to remember the colors and their order is to use the mnemonic name ROY G BV. Each letter stands for the first letter of each of the rainbow colors. (Indigo used to be considered part of the spectrum. Many scientists now regard it as a blended color of blue and violet.) Red, yellow, and blue are the primary colors. When blended together in different combinations, they form the secondary colors, orange, green, and violet. Note: In this activity, students mix colors using transparent colored plastic. Because this material transmits light, students are technically exploring the primary colors of light (which differ from primary colors). However, when students overlap the red, yellow, and blue strips they will see orange, green, and violet. Simply explain that these are primary pigments, instead of colors.

Invite students to compare the quartet of poems titled "Four Poems for Roy G Biv" in Barbara Juster Esbenson's *Who Shrank My Grandmother's House? Poems of Discovery* (HarperCollins, 1992). Each poem explores rainbows from a different poetic perspective.

Materials

red, yellow, and blue transparent plastic sheets, cut into 1-by-6-inch strips (report covers work well) (4 strips of each color per student)

scissors

tape

colored construction paper or tagboard

1 Ask students if they have ever seen rainbows. If so, where? (through a drinking glass or a prism, after a sun shower, above the spray of a sprinkler, on a compact disc or a soap bubble) Ask: What colors do you think are in a rainbow? Show students photographs or pictures of rainbows and help them identify the colors they see.

2 Hand out a red, yellow, and blue plastic strip to each student. Explain that these are called primary pigments. Challenge students to create rainbow colors using these three pigments. Give students time to explore overlapping the strips in different ways.

3 Ask students to describe what colors they can make with the strips. (overlap yellow and blue to make green; red and yellow to make orange; blue and red to make violet) Explain that when they mix primary pigments in this way, they create new colors called secondary pigments.

4 Distribute 9 more strips (3 each of red, yellow, blue). Students will need 12 strips in all. Show them how to use them to create a rainbowlike checkerboard design.

- On a white surface, lay 6 strips side by side vertically, alternating red, yellow, and blue strips.

- Carefully tape the ends of the strips together.

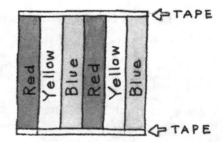

- Lay 6 more strips horizontally on top of the first set of strips. Begin with red and alternate the colors as before to create a square.

- Tape the ends together to hold the strips in place.

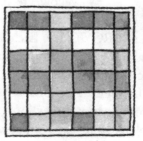

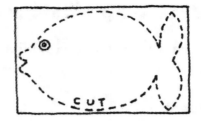

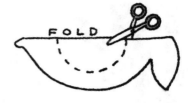

5 Have each student cut out a construction paper or tagboard fish (or another animal or shape). Show how to fold the fish in half, cut out a half circle or abstract shape from the middle, and unfold.

6 Let students glue or tape the rainbow designs to the back of the fish so the colors show through the opening, then cut off any excess. Tape fish to a window and watch them catch the light!

V A R I A T I O N

COLOR MIXING: Make other kinds of mixed-color designs. For blue-green ocean waves for the fish to swim in, cut out and overlap wave shapes from blue and yellow plastic. For spectacular sunsets, cut out red and yellow suns as well as red, yellow, and blue cloud shapes. Overlap them in different ways to create unusual effects. For rainbows, cut arc shapes from colored plastic and overlap them so the colors appear in the correct order.

TIP Here's a fun and easy way to display these designs in your window and teach a quick lesson on static electricity (see page 102). On a dry day, have students rub the plastic shapes on their hair or a wool sweater, then press them onto the glass. Static electricity charges will make the shapes hold on tight!

To demonstrate adhesion at work, wet the back of the plastic shapes with water and press them to the glass. They will stick until the water evaporates.

Primary Color Peacock Fans

Students experiment with mixing primary colors to make secondary colors when they create colorful peacock fans.

Materials
newspaper
white craft paper, 11 by 17 inches (1 piece per student)
red, yellow, and blue tempera paints
     (thinned with a little water)
paintbrushes
water
smocks
peacock pattern (below)
stapler
scissors
glue
markers or crayons

1 Spread newspaper on students' work surfaces. Hand out copies of the peacock pattern, scissors, white paper, paints, water, and paintbrushes. Write the color pattern illustrated below on the board (or make and display a sample) for students to copy.

2 Have students brush plain water over their papers, then make their peacock fans.

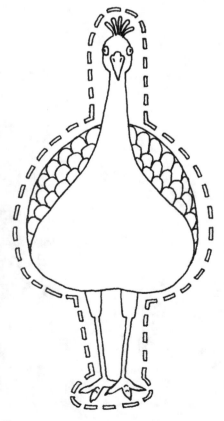

Peacock pattern

- Paint 12 to 15 thin stripes of red, yellow, and blue on your paper. (The stripes can touch.)

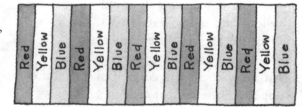

- Fold the paper in half the long way (painted side in) and place the paper on a work surface. Gently rub the top side with your hand then turn the paper over and rub again.

- Carefully peel apart the two halves. What colors do you see? (Folding the paper mixes the colors, creating the secondary colors orange, green, and violet.)

- When the paint is dry, make a 1-inch fold along one of the short ends of the paper. Make another fold in the opposite direction. Continue making these accordion folds until you reach the end of the paper.

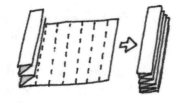

- Cut one end of the folded paper to make a pointy tail shape. Staple the folds together at the other end. Open the pointy end to make the peacock's tail.

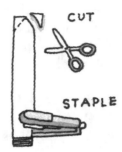

- Cut out the peacock pattern and color it. Glue it to the front of the fan.

• • • • • V A R I A T I O N • • • • •

TISSUE-PAPER FANS: Instead of paint, use overlapping strips of colored tissue paper. First brush the white paper with school glue that has been thinned with water. Lay down the strips and brush again with glue. Let dry. Then make the fans as directed above.

Pointillist Paintings

Students explore how our eyes and brain blend small dots of color to make new colors.

Materials
magazines with colorful pictures, color comic strips
hand lenses
paints
fine paintbrushes or cotton swabs
pencils
paper
art books or postcards with examples of artwork by
pointillist painters Georges Seurat, Paul Signac, or Camille Pissarro

Learn more about pointillism by sharing *Paintings* by Claude Delafosse and Gallimard Jeunesse (Scholastic, 1993). Part of the First Discovery Art Book series, this colorful book includes examples of artwork by the famous pointillist painter, Georges Seurat. To explore his style, readers see both close-up and pulled-back views of his paintings. For other examples of pointillism, check your library for art books about Neo-Impressionism.

1 Invite students to look at various printed photos and illustrations and describe the colors they see.

2 Let them examine the same pictures with hand lenses. What colors do they see now? (tiny cyan [blue], magenta [hot pink], yellow, and black dots) Some of these dots overlap; some are side by side. Explain that pictures in printed matter are created using only these four colors. When we look at a picture without a magnifier, the dots are too small for our eyes and brain to separate. Instead, the colors seem to blend together to create an array of different colors.

3 Invite students to study examples of pointillist artwork. (See Book Break, left.) Have them describe the effects artists create by using tiny dots of different colors of paint.

4 Have students create their own pointillist paintings using dots of paint applied with fine paintbrushes or cotton swabs. It will be easier for students if they first sketch the outline of their picture with a pencil, outline it with dots of paint, then fill it in with more dots. Let them experiment with using dots of primary colors to create secondary colors, making different-sized dots, and so on. Remind students to use a different cotton swab for each color.

TIP Have students mix black paint into their colors to make darker tones, white paint for lighter tones. Students can add dark or light highlights by layering dark and light dots over the colored dots already on their papers.

5 Display students' paintings and discuss the effect this dot-by-dot technique creates!

• • • EXTENSION • • •

Hidden Colors: Hold up a magnifier to a TV screen (turn it on) to discover that every colorful electronic picture is made up of thin strips of just three colors—blue, green, and red. That's because televisions and computers use light beams, not pigments. The primary colors of light are blue, green, and red.

Colorful Kaleidoscopes

Students explore the science of reflection by making simple kaleidoscopes.

▲▲▲▲▲▲▲▲▲▲▲▲▲▲▲▲▲▲▲▲▲▲▲▲▲

SCIENCE TALK

▲▲▲▲▲▲▲▲▲▲▲▲▲▲▲▲▲▲▲▲▲▲▲▲▲

A kaleidoscope creates the effect that there are many more objects than there really are. Mirrors *reflect* or bounce images of the objects back and forth, creating multiple, repeating images and patterns.

Materials

small square or rectangular mirrors, same size
   (3 per student; see Supply Sources, page 9, and Tip, page 80)
masking tape
small objects such as pennies or paper clips
markers
plastic wrap
scissors
rubber bands
small colored beads, seeds, colored confetti, sequins, glitter,
   or colored tissue paper cut into tiny pieces
decorative paper such as gift wrap scraps
Colorful Kaleidoscopes journal page (page 89)

1 Have each student place two mirrors side by side, facedown on a work space. Show students how to tape the backs of the mirrors together, leaving a tiny space between them. This will allow the mirrors to bend after they are taped. Tell students to cut off any extra tape.

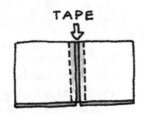

TAPE
⇩

2 MIRRORS
FACEDOWN

2 Hand out the journal page. Have students line up the mirrors on top of the first set of lines and place a small object such as a paper clip or a penny in front of the mirrors. How many images or reflections of the object do they see? (four)

3 Next, ask students to predict how many reflections they will see when they stand the mirrors on the lines in number 2. Then have them test to find out. (six)

4 Have students move the mirrors closer together and farther apart. How does this change the number of reflections they see? (farther apart, fewer images; closer together, a greater number)

5 Have students complete number 3 on the journal page (color designs on the circle) and pair up for the next step. (If they like, students can cut out the circle.) While one student holds the mirrors in place on the center of the circle, the other can turn the page and observe the reflections.

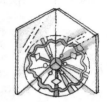

6 Invite students to share their observations. (The part of the design that faces the mirrors is reflected, creating a different, but complete, circle design in the glass.)

7 Next have students make kaleidoscopes.

- Lay the two mirrors facedown again. Tape on a third mirror. Stand them up and fold them inward to make a triangle. The mirror sides should be on the inside. Tape the third side closed.

- Cut a piece of plastic wrap slightly bigger than the opening of the triangle. Put it over the opening and use a rubber band to hold it in place. The plastic wrap should be flat and tight. Tape it in place.

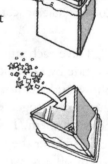

- Turn the kaleidoscope over so the plastic wrap is on the bottom. Sprinkle a few tiny beads or paper stars, and some glitter onto the plastic wrap.

- Tape decorative paper around the outside of the kaleidoscope.

8 Have students look inside their kaleidoscopes. What do they see? Encourage them to experiment with moving their kaleidoscopes in different ways. For example, what happens when they let light shine in from the bottom or turn their kaleidoscopes so that the colored objects move around?

TIP If you have a limited number of mirrors, divide students into groups and have them do the activity at different times. You can also substitute Mylar (although the images will be distorted and not as clear as mirror reflections). Glue pieces of Mylar to cardboard squares. Smooth out wrinkles, trim off excess, and let dry. Then assemble the kaleidoscope as directed above.

Shimmery Color Bursts

Students explore iridescence by making ornaments that shimmer and shine.

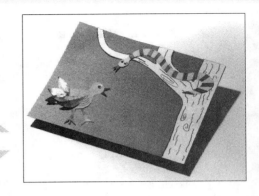

SCIENCE TALK

In this activity, nail polish and water combine to create shimmering *iridescent* colors on paper. The lustrous swirling rainbow of colors that appears is the result of the polish breaking up white light (just like a prism or a soap bubble does). What causes the varying patterns of colors? The polish doesn't spread out evenly on the paper. The colors that appear in different spots depend on the thickness of the polish there.

Materials (for each group)

newspaper
foil pie plates
nickels
black, dark blue, or purple construction paper, cut into 4-inch squares
water
clear nail polish
facial tissues

1 Divide students into groups. Cover each group's work surface with newspapers. Give each group a pie plate, a nickel, and the squares of dark paper. Have each group fill the pie plate with water, then set it on the newspaper.

2 One at a time, have students slide a square of paper into the water then place a nickel on the center of the paper. (This will keep the paper from floating up.)

3 Stop by each group and let a drop of nail polish drip off the brush into the water. Ask students to observe what happens to the drop as it hits the water. (It spreads out and a rainbowlike film forms on the water's surface.) Have students gently and slowly pull their papers out of the water, letting the nickels slip off. What do they observe? (a rainbowlike iridescent layer on the surface of the paper)

BOOK BREAK

After students make their Shimmery Color Bursts, share *Rainbow Crow: A Lenape Tale* by Nancy Van Laan (Knopf, 1989). This Native American folktale explains how Crow got his iridescent feathers that shine with all of the colors of the rainbow.

TIP Before the next round of students take their turns, use a tissue to remove any of the remaining nail polish film from the water. Again, stop by each group to add a drop of nail polish to the water.

4 Have students set their papers on newspaper to dry. When dry, students will enjoy making a variety of decorative projects with their shimmery paper. See Variations, below.

• • • VARIATIONS • • •

SHIMMERY CREATURES: Cut out butterflies, snakes, or birds from construction paper, draw on features with crayons, then cut up the shimmery paper to make scales or feathers and glue them on.

BRILLIANT BOOKMARKS: Use construction paper strips instead of squares to make iridescent bookmarks.

SHIMMERY GIFT WRAP: Cut up the iridescent paper into various small shapes and glue to colored tissue paper to make festive gift wrap.

Stained-Glass Surprises

Students explore the concept of translucence by making crayon stained glass.

SCIENCE TALK

When light hits an object, it is either transmitted, reflected, or absorbed. Transparent objects, such as a glass window or clear plastic wrap, transmit light. Mirrors reflect light. Translucent objects, such as waxed or tissue paper and frosted glass, transmit some of the light and reflect the rest. Opaque objects, such as wood, totally block light. In this activity, students observe how oil on crayon-colored paper creates translucent paper with a stained-glass effect. How does oil make paper translucent? When oil saturates paper, a porous material, its molecules move between the particles of the paper. As a transparent liquid, the oil then transmits light through the paper.

Materials
Stained-Glass Surprises pattern page (page 90)
crayons
scissors
cooking oil
paper cups
cotton balls
tape

1 Ask students if they know what people used for windows before glass was invented. Explain that long ago, people often used greased animal skins or oiled paper as windowpanes.

2 Hand out the pattern page and invite students to color the design any way they wish—or use it as a model for creating their own. Tell them to press firmly and fill in all the white spaces, then cut out their designs. Color an extra design to serve as a basis of comparison for students' oiled designs.

3 Set out a few cups of oil for students to share. Let them rub a cotton ball dipped in oil over their designs, then set them in a place to dry overnight. Don't oil the extra picture you colored.

4 The next day, tape students' pictures to a window, oil side to the glass. Tape up the un-oiled picture as well. Have students compare the amount of light that passes through the oiled and un-oiled papers. Ask: What do you think the oil did to the paper? (It soaked into it, making the paper translucent and allowing some light to pass through.)

Help students appreciate the beauty of stained glass by sharing *The Story of Stained Glass* by Nancy E. Krulik, included in Scholastic's Creativity Zone Stained Glass Craft Kit (Scholastic, 1996). This book explains how stained-glass windows are created and explores the history of this art form through beautiful color photographs. The book also includes easy-to-do activities and a small packet of materials.

VARIATIONS

STAINED-GLASS LOOK-ALIKES: For a different effect, try these techniques.

- Paint a design with oil on a piece of paper, then brush watercolor or thinned tempera paints over and around the design. When the paint dries, glue on black construction paper windowpanes (arches, squares, etc.).

- Create the effect of the leaded panes in some stained-glass windows. Make a mixture of equal parts black tempera paint and school glue. Squirt or paint thin lines on paper where you want the "lead" to appear. When the paint-and-glue mixture dries, use crayon and oil to fill in the colored part of the "glass."

- Make spooky pumpkins for Halloween fun. Draw a pumpkin with crayon on a white or brown paper lunch bag (upside down), then brush with oil. Make cuts for eyes, a nose, and a mouth. Stand a flashlight on end inside the bag. Darken the room and turn on the flashlight for an eerie effect!

Shadow Silhouettes

Students explore the properties of shadows as they create portraits of one another.

SCIENCE TALK

Light travels in a straight line. When it hits a three-dimensional object, the light is blocked, and a two-dimensional shadow of the object appears on a wall or other flat surface. The closer an object is to the light source, the larger and fuzzier its shadow will be. When an object is farther away from the light, its shadow will be smaller and sharper.

Materials

lamp

chair

large pieces of dark blue, purple, or black construction paper (1 per student)

tape

white crayons

scissors

large pieces of white construction paper (1 per student)

glue

1 Darken the room and shine a strong light source on the wall. Place a chair sideways next to the wall and ask a student volunteer to take the seat. Adjust the position of the light until a clear, sharp shadow of the student's profile appears on the wall.

2 Ask students to describe what they observe. (a dark outline of the student's face, called a shadow) Then ask them to describe how the shadow is different from the student's face. (The shadow doesn't show any of the student's features; it's flat compared to the student's three-dimensional head.)

3 Invite students to work in pairs to make shadow portraits.

- Student A sits sideways in a chair between the wall and the lamp, as shown in step 2.

- Student B tapes a piece of dark construction paper to the wall so the partner's profile appears on the paper.

- Student B uses a white crayon to draw the outline of the partner's profile on the dark paper.

- Student B cuts out the image, mounts it on a piece of white paper and, as the portrait artist, signs the back.

- Students then swap roles.

4 When everyone has made a portrait, display students' work. Challenge students to match portraits with people.

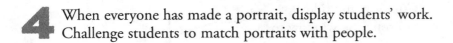

• • • VARIATIONS • • •

MYSTERY SHADOWS: Make and display mystery portraits of objects such as keys, scissors, or feathers. Who can match objects with portraits?

SHADOWS PATTERNS: Try tracing the silhouettes of other objects, such as animal figurines, leaves, or hands. Cut out multiple copies of each and use negative and positive space to create repeating patterns.

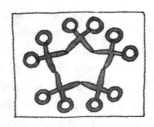

BOOK BREAK

Shadows and Reflections by Tana Hoban (Greenwillow, 1990), a wordless book illustrated with exquisite photographs, depicts shadows and reflections created by familiar objects.

Invite students to discover how negative and positive space can be used to achieve different effects by sharing *Round Trip* by Ann Jonas (Greenwillow, 1983), an unusual book that can be read forward, backward, and upside down.

Shadow Show

Students produce shadow puppet shows to explore the science behind these light shows.

Materials

cardboard box (the larger the better)
scissors
waxed paper
tape
pushpins
fabric
decorating materials (paint, glitter, stickers, fabric or wallpaper scraps)
thin cardboard
straws or unsharpened pencils
clear plastic
lamp or flashlight

1 First have students make a theater for their puppet shows.

- Cut a window in the side of a large box. (A large appliance box allows for a lot of puppet action in the theater.) Make the window as large as you want the stage to be. Cut away the side opposite the window to create a large opening.

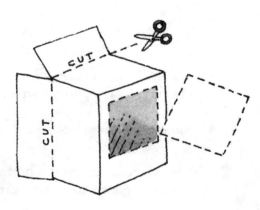

- Tape waxed paper over the opening. If you need more than one sheet of waxed paper to cover the window, tape one piece to the window top, bottom, and side first, then butt the edge of a second piece up against the first so that the seam does not overlap before taping in place.

- Decorate the stage. Add a curtain by draping a piece of fabric around the waxed paper. Use pushpins to hold it in place.

2 Show students how to make puppets out of cardboard. Cut out the basic shape first, then use a pencil to poke holes for eyes or scissors to snip out other features. Tape the puppets to straws or unsharpened pencils.

3 Darken the room. Turn on the lamp and direct it from behind at the waxed paper screen. Have students predict what will happen when they hold the puppets between the light and the waxed paper screen. Let them test their ideas and share what they observe. (The cardboard puppets will make shadows on the screen. This happens because the cardboard is opaque and blocks light.) Let students predict what will happen to the shadows if they move their puppets close to the light, then farther away. Can students make their puppets change shape? Have them turn the puppets in various ways.

SAFETY NOTE

Make sure the light cord is safely out of the way or taped down. Go over safety rules. If you use a flashlight instead, students can take turns holding it while others manipulate their puppets.

Shadowgraphs Anyone Can Make (Running Press, 1991) shows easy-to-understand hand puppet positions and offers neat ideas for puppet performances.

Hand Shadows

Duck

Spider

Dog

4 Let students experiment with using a transparent object, such as a clear plastic report cover, to make shadows. Light passes through the clear plastic and does not make a shadow. Review with students what makes a shadow (a source of light, an object to make a shadow, and a surface on which to cast the shadow).

5 Invite students to work in small groups to plan and produce puppet shows. Familiar stories, such as the Three Little Pigs, are fun to act out. Other ideas include acting out class problems, or writing and scripting original stories. Invite a younger class to the show!

• • • • V A R I A T I O N S • • • •

CHANGING COLORS: Explore more elaborate shadow effects. For example, to make colored shadows, use colored cellophane instead of the waxed paper for the screen, or a colored lightbulb in the lamp.

CULTURE CONNECTION: Research the art of Indonesian shadow puppets that have moving parts. To make them, draw puppet parts on thin cardboard, then cut them out. Connect the parts with brass paper fasteners. Tape long sticks, such as dowels (or tape together pencils, end to end) to each moving part of the puppet body. Manipulate the puppet by moving the sticks in different ways.

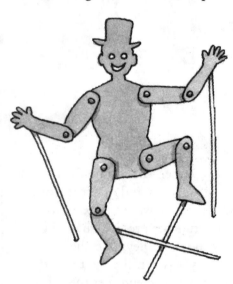

HAND SHADOWS: Make moving pictures with your hands. See the sample hand positions, at left. Darken the room and shine a lamp on the wall. Place your hand between the light source and the wall and make your hand puppets move!

Name _____

Colorful Kaleidoscopes

1. Line up and stand the mirrors on this pattern. Place a small object in front of the mirrors. How many objects do you see in the mirrors?

_____

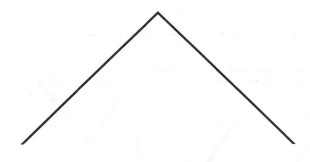

2. Stand the mirrors on this pattern. Place a small object in front of the mirrors. How many objects do you see now?

_____

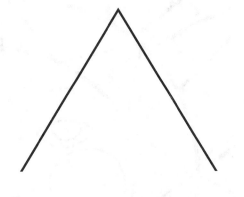

3. Use different colored crayons or markers to color a design on this circle. Make different shapes and patterns.

4. Ask a friend to place the two mirrors on the center of the circle. While your friend holds the mirrors, turn this page in a circle. What happens to your design?

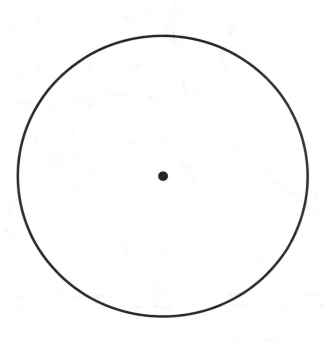

ScienceART Scholastic Professional Books

Stained-Glass Surprises

Exploring Energy

Pinwheels whirl…chimes jingle…
mini-merry-go-rounds spin…
battery-operated fireflies flash…
What do these art projects have in common?
Energy. In our everyday lives, energy is what
lets laundry dry on a line, sends sounds our
way, and keeps lights lit. In this chapter,
students explore different kinds of energy
and the way it is stored or used.

Stored Energy

These first two activities let students explore *potential* or *stored energy*
and *kinetic energy*. An object has potential energy when it is capable of
moving or causing other objects to move. A rock on top of a hill and a
compressed spring are examples of objects with potential energy. This
energy becomes kinetic once the energy is released and the object is in
motion.

Pop-up Coil Cards

Students explore ways to use stored energy to make pop-up
greeting cards that are fun for any occasion.

SCIENCE TALK

When you close the lid on a jack-in-the-box, you're using
energy to compress the spring. The energy is then stored
by the spring as potential energy. Opening the lid releases
this energy as kinetic energy. As the spring pops up, it
pushes open the lid and extends the jack-in-the-box.
Students apply this concept when they make greeting cards with paper
springs inside.

Materials

various kinds of springs (from pens, flashlights)
lightweight cardboard strips, each about 1 by 12 inches
   (old file folders work well) (2 per student)
glue
construction paper
assorted art supplies such as glitter and markers
scissors
tape or paper clips

1 Pass around different kinds of springs for students to examine and explore how they work. Ask: What do you think the coils in a spring do? (When the coils are compressed, they hold stored or potential energy. When the coils are released, the stored energy becomes active or kinetic energy as the spring pops up.)

2 Show students how to make their own springs out of cardboard.

- Glue together the ends of two strips. They should form an L shape. Let the glue dry.

- Fold the strip on the bottom over the strip on top and make a crease. Continue overlapping the strips until they are completely folded. Glue down the last flap.

- Hold the spring between your fingers and compress. Then let it go at the top. Is your spring springy?

3 Invite students to draw pictures and/or write greetings on one end of their springs (or cut one out of colored paper and glue it on). Then have them fold a piece of construction paper in half, decorate the outside, and glue the other end of their springs to the inside.

TIP To keep cards closed until recipients open them, place a small piece of tape along the open side or fasten with a paper clip.

4 When the glue is dry, let students test their pop-ups by closing and opening their cards. What happens? (The spring pops up.)

• • • • VARIATION • • • •

MAKE "JACK-IN-THE-BOX" TOYS: Glue a spring to the bottom of a small jewelry box, such as one that pins or earrings come in. Glue a jack-in-the box picture on the end of the spring, then cover the box with the lid. When the lid is removed, the "jack" will pop up.

Windup Whirligigs

Students make mini-merry-go-rounds
to discover how stored energy can make things move.

Materials (for each student)

several medium rubber bands
2 crayons
small cylinder-shaped oatmeal box
construction paper
dessert-size paper plate
tape
several whirligig patterns (page 95)
assorted art supplies (markers, crayons, glitter, stickers)
pencils
toothpicks
twist tie from plastic bags
Life Saver candy (use Pepomint, other kinds get sticky)
ribbon or yarn
scissors

SCIENCE TALK

In this activity, students construct a simple windup toy. What makes the whirligig spin? Students use energy when they turn the crayon and wind up the rubber band inside the box. The rubber band stores this energy. When the crayon is released, the energy becomes active or kinetic and is transferred to the paper plate. The plate then turns on the Life Saver. (The Life Saver helps to reduce *friction* between the plate and the lid of the box. Friction is the rubbing between surfaces that causes objects in motion to slow down.)

1 Give each student a rubber band and two crayons. Have students wrap the crayons loosely with their rubber bands, set them on their desks, and observe what happens. (nothing)

2 Now ask students to twist the crayons to wind up the rubber band tightly, then set the crayons on their desks without letting go. When you say "Go!" students quickly pull away their hands. What happens? (The crayons dance around on the desk.)

3 Discuss what made the crayons dance. (Students supplied the energy when they twisted the crayons; the rubber bands stored this energy. The stored energy became active when students released the wound-up crayons.)

4 Tell students they are going to make toys that run on rubber band power. Have them gather a set of materials, then follow these steps.

TIP Putting the whirligigs together can be a bit tricky. Prepare a model in advance to guide students in making their own. Also, as students follow your directions, make another along with them to demonstrate each step.

- Cover the box with construction paper, tape in place, and decorate. Also decorate the paper plate. Copy, color, and cut out several carousel horses (page 95).

TIP A colorful spiral design on the paper plate creates a great effect when the plate spins.

- Use a pencil point to poke a hole in the middle of the bottom of the box. Poke a rubber band most of the way through the hole.

- Slip a toothpick through the end of the rubber band that sticks out of the box. Pull the rubber band from the inside of the box so that the toothpick is flush with the box. Tape it in place.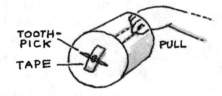

- Poke a hole in the middle of the lid and the paper plate. Use a bent twist tie to pull the rubber band through the box and through the hole in the lid.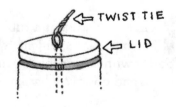

- Use the twist tie to thread the rubber band through the Life Saver (rough side down) then through the plate (curved side up). Slip the crayon through the rubber band to hold it in place. Remove the twist tie.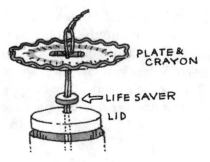

- Tape each carousel horse to a five-inch length of ribbon or yarn. Tape the other end of each under the rim of the plate, so the animals hang down. (Or poke holes around the edge of the plate and tie them on.)

- To wind up the whirligig, hold the box with one hand and use the index finger on the other to turn the crayon around and around in the same direction, stopping when you feel some resistance.

- Ready, set, whirl! Let go of the crayon and watch the whirligig spin.

TIP If students' rubber bands are too long, have them tie knots to shorten them or use shorter rubber bands to assemble the whirligigs. (This will decrease the amount they need to turn the crayon to build up resistance in the rubber band.)

5 Have students wind up their whirligigs again, this time counting the number of turns they give the crayons and the number of spins when they let go. Then ask students to record in their science journals what makes the whirligigs spin. (Turning the crayon winds up the rubber band, which stores the energy. This energy becomes active when the crayon is released. The energy then gets transferred to the plate. The plate turns on the Life Saver, which helps to reduce friction or rubbing between the plate and the lid.)

TIP After a number of spins, the rubber bands may get stretched out or fray and break. Have students replace them with fresh rubber bands.

Whirligig pattern

Air & Wind

You can't see it, but it surrounds our planet, this mixture of nitrogen, oxygen, carbon dioxide, water vapor, and other substances. It's air! Moving air is called wind. With the set of activities here, students will explore air and wind as sources of energy.

Air Power Pop-ups

Students discover that air takes up space and that moving air can exert force and do work.

Materials (for each student)
empty, narrow cardboard tea box (Celestial Seasonings boxes work well)
balloon
pencil
bathroom tissue tube
assorted art supplies (felt, colored construction paper, wiggly eyes, paints and brushes)
tape
scissors

1 Before students begin, give them each a balloon and have them try this.

- Place your hand on top of the balloon, near the edge of the desk.

- Blow up the balloon. What happens? (Their hand lifts up.) Why? (Energy from their lungs filled the balloon with air; because air takes up space, the inflated balloon lifted their hand.)

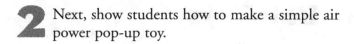

2 Next, show students how to make a simple air power pop-up toy.

- Make two cuts in one end of the box, then trim the flap (as shown). This will become the top of the box out of which the toy will pop.

- Tape closed the original opening to the box.

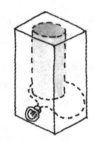

- Use a pencil to poke a hole in the front of the box, near the bottom.

- Put the balloon inside the box and carefully pull out the open end through the hole.

TIP Let students stretch and blow up their balloons (then let out the air) before putting them in the boxes and through the holes. This will make it easier to blow them up when they're inside the box with the tube on top.

- Set the cardboard tube inside the box and close the top.

- Blow into the balloon through the open end. What happens? (Blowing into the balloon causes it to inflate within the narrow confines of the box. This in turn makes the cardboard tube pop up.)

3 Let students decorate their boxes and cardboard tubes in creative ways, such as making a mouse that peeks out of its hole, a circus acrobat that shoots out of a cannon, a groundhog that peeks out of a burrow, or a cupid that pops up to send heartfelt greetings on Valentine's Day!

BOOK BREAK

Introduce this book by asking: How could you get rid of all the pesky problem makers in your life—for example, your teacher, your toothbrush, or your mom's piano? Balloons and air power provide the answer in *I'm Flying!* by Alan Wade (Knopf, 1990).

For another amusing look at air power, share *The Grumpalump* by Sarah Hayes (Clarion, 1990), a hilarious rhyming romp that recounts the misguided efforts of a group of animals trying to get a hot air balloon off the ground.

EXTENSIONS

Toy Designer Teams: Form teams to design other toys, games, and greeting cards that use air power to make their parts move.

Air Power at Work: Research other moving things that use air power as an energy source (airplanes, kites, sailboats, windmills, hot air balloons).

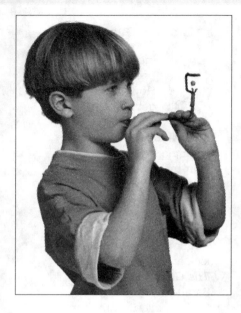

Floating Ball Toys

Students discover that moving air can exert a force when they make these air powered toys.

This toy is a copy of the nineteenth-century floating ball, a penny toy that challenged the user to suspend a cork ball or dried pea on a stream of air blown though a pipe or tube. In this adaptation, the stream of air that comes out of the straw rushes around the "ball," traps it, and keeps it suspended.

Materials (for each student)
flexible plastic straw
pipe cleaner
scissors
dried chickpeas or ball-shaped cereal such as Kix

1 Show students how to assemble and play with their toys.

- Make four cuts in the bendable end of the straw. Bend back the pieces to make a basket.

- Cut a piece of pipe cleaner about seven inches long. Make a bend in it as shown. Then bend the rest of it to make a hoop.

- Tape the hoop to the straw so it sits about one inch above the basket. Bend the straw at the flexible end.

- To play, set a ball (dried chickpea or piece of Kix cereal) in the basket and blow through the straw. Try to make the ball lift up and drop back in the basket. Try to make the ball lift up through the hoop too.

2 Ask: What happens when you blow through the straw? (The ball lifts up.) What makes this happen? (Blowing into the straw creates a stream of moving air that lifts the ball.) What would happen if you made your straw shorter? Would it be harder or easier to lift the ball? Let students experiment to find out. (A shorter straw takes less breath to lift the ball.)

Warm Air Whirlers

Students use the energy from warm air to make paper flowers whirl around—and in the process, discover what makes winds.

Warm air is lighter than cold air. As the air above a lamp or radiator warms, it rises. The surrounding heavier, cooler air moves in to take its place and pushes up on the warm air. This creates air currents that, in this activity, push against the flaps on the flowers, causing them to spin. Winds are created in the same way.

Materials

Warm Air Whirler pattern (page 116)
scissors
crayons or markers
pencil
thread
lamp or radiator

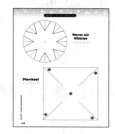

1 Hand out the pattern and have students make their flowers.

- Cut out the circle shape, then color or decorate it.

- Make cuts along the eight dotted lines, then make folds along the solid lines, alternating them so that one faces up, the next down, and so on.

- Use a pencil point to make a hole in the flower's center. Poke a piece of thread through the hole and make a knot so the flower hangs at the end of the thread.

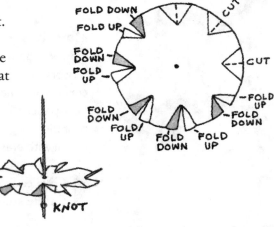

2 Have students hold their flowers by the thread. Do they spin? (No. They hang straight down.) Ask students to predict what will happen when they hang them over a heat source.

3 Have students take turns holding their flowers about six inches above a lamp or radiator, away from drafts. Ask them to stand as still as possible to avoid creating air currents that might affect the results. What happens? (The flowers whirl around.)

SAFETY NOTE

Supervise students closely to make sure the paper flowers do not get too close to the heat source.

99

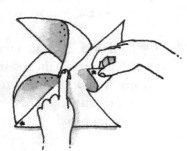

4 Challenge students to think of ways to improve their designs for more dramatic effects.

- Make the flaps bigger or smaller.

- Turn the flaps in different directions.

- Try making flowers out of other materials such as tissue paper, aluminum foil, waxed paper, iridescent paper (see page 81), or the colorful paper from the Butterfly Symmetry activity (see page 31).

• • • • • VARIATIONS • • • • •

WARM AIR MOBILES: For a dramatic effect, put flowers together to make a warm air powered mobile. (See the Starry Sky Mobiles activity on page 123. Substitute lengths of thread for the paper clip chains.)

WACKY WHIRLYBIRDS: Turn the flowers into wacky whirlybirds by drawing on eyes and beaks and gluing craft feathers to the flaps.

Pinwheel Power

With this familiar toy, students observe the wind at work.

Materials (for each student)
Pinwheel pattern (page 116)
scissors
crayons and markers
newspaper
pushpin
pencil with eraser

1 Give each student a copy of the pattern. Guide students to put the pinwheels together.

- Cut out the square. Decorate the pinwheel pattern on both sides and cut along the dotted lines.

- Place the pattern on a work surface on top of a piece of folded newspaper. Bring each corner with a star into the center. Make sure the stars all line up, one on top of another. Hold the corners in place with your finger.

- Push a pin through the stars, being careful not to crease the paper blades.

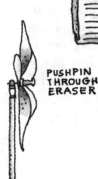

PUSHPIN THROUGH ERASER

- Push the pin into the side of a pencil eraser.

2 Invite students to blow on their pinwheels. Use these questions to guide an exploration of wind power. Have students record predictions and observations in their science journals.

- What makes your pinwheel turn? (Moving air from students' breath pushes on the cupped part of the blades.)

- Does it matter how hard you blow or where you aim your breath? Try from the side, from the front, and so on.

- What if you flattened the blades of your pinwheel? How would this affect its turning power?

- Does it matter how far the pushpin sticks into the eraser?

- What if you put the pinwheel on top of the eraser instead of on the side?

 TIP Have extra pinwheel patterns and pencils on hand for students to experiment with making changes to the basic design.

VARIATIONS

ON THE MOVE: Use pinwheels outdoors to measure the wind's strength and direction. Compare how fast the pinwheels move on different days by counting and recording how many times the pinwheels turn in 10 seconds. Also observe which way the pinwheels turn.

DOUBLE PINWHEEL POWER: Would a pinwheel with more blades work differently? Join together two pinwheel patterns and attach them to the pencil eraser to find out.

PINWHEEL TOWER: Tape together three pencils with erasers, end to end, then attach a pinwheel to each eraser. Investigate the effect of placing the pinwheels so each faces a different direction.

Electricity

Electricity is a form of energy that can be turned into light, heat, and power. How many ways each day do we experience electricity? From the static electricity that makes our hair stand straight up to the current electricity that lights our homes and the chemical electricity in batteries that makes portable radios play, this form of energy is all around. The activities that follow let students safely experiment with electricity to see how it works.

Snake Charmers

Students explore static electricity by bringing yarn snakes to life!

SCIENCE TALK

Many different kinds of materials when rubbed together create *static electricity*—a harmless form of electrical energy. Static electricity causes the slight spark and harmless shock when you touch a metal doorknob after walking across a rug or pulling off a wool sweater in winter. These shocks occur as we discharge static electricity that accumulates on our bodies. Static electricity also creates the lightning bolts we see during a thunderstorm. As a storm cloud grows, particles inside become electrically charged. Negative and positive charges build up in different parts of the cloud. Finally, this built-up static electricity discharges to another cloud or to a tall object on the ground, such as a tree, creating a flash of lightning.

Materials (for each student)

6-inch-long pieces of yarn
tape
tissue paper (optional)
glue (optional)
small basket (optional)
balloon

TIP This activity works best on a day with low humidity. Water in the air increases the air's conductivity and prevents static buildup.

1 Have each student make a snake by taping one end of a piece of yarn to a desk. For fun, students can tape the end of the yarn inside a small basket instead. And if they like, they can decorate tissue-paper heads and glue them to the other end of the yarn.

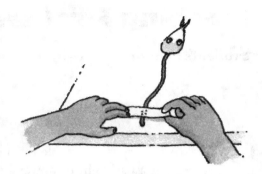

BOOK BREAK

Explore the static electricity that creates lightning with *Rumble Thumble Boom* by Anna Grossnickle Hines (Greenwillow, 1992), a story that may inspire students to discuss their feelings about thunderstorms— and ways they handle their fears.

2 Next, ask students to blow up balloons, tie them closed, then rub them against their hair. Ask: What do you notice when you rub the balloon against your hair? (Their hair stands up. The act of rubbing the balloon and the hair causes both to become electrically charged. Strands of hair become attracted to the balloon. Explain that this creates static electricity.) Ask students if they can think of other times they've experienced static electricity. (taking clothes out of the dryer, combing their hair, touching a doorknob or a person after walking across a carpet and getting a shock)

3 Now let students become snake charmers! Challenge them to use their balloons to make their snakes dance. They can charge their balloons by rubbing them against their hair, then holding them a few inches above their snakes and moving them gently. The charged balloons attract the uncharged yarn snakes, lifting them off the desk.

4 Ask: What other materials might make static electricity? Invite students to experiment rubbing objects such as plastic or rubber combs against hair, wool, nylon, and other materials, then record observations in their science journals.

● ● ● ● ● ● ● **VARIATION** ● ● ● ● ● ● ●

STATIC ELECTRICITY SNOWSTORM: For a winter snow scene, cut out tiny tissue paper snowflakes, place them in a clear plastic deli container with a lid, and use a charged balloon to make a whirling snowstorm. What other ways can students make static electricity work?

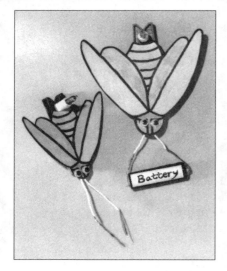

Flashing Fireflies

Students light up fireflies by making simple electrical circuits.

SCIENCE TALK

A battery is a portable form of chemical energy that can light a flashlight or power a smoke detector. To produce electricity, a battery needs something that uses electricity (like a bulb) and a pathway or *closed circuit* to travel through. Materials that electricity can travel through, such as metal and water, are called *conductors*.

SAFETY NOTE

The electricity produced by the batteries in these investigations is safe for students to work with. Though students may report feeling heat from the batteries, the electricity is not strong enough to cause a shock. Make sure students understand that although the electricity in batteries is safe to handle, it is very different from other forms of electricity used in school and at home. Students should never experiment with electrical outlets, lamps, electrical appliances, or switches. In addition, these devices should never be used near water or with wet hands because water conducts electricity.

Materials

miniature holiday tree lights, cut into 6-inch strips with one bulb in each (1 per student) (see Tip, page 105)

wire stripper

firefly pattern (below)

scissors

spring-type clothespins (1 per student)

glue

tape

decorating materials (markers, sequins, wiggly eyes)

AA batteries (1 per student)

Flashing Firefly journal page (page 117)

materials that conduct electricity (aluminum foil, metal spoons, paper clips, nails, keys)

materials that don't conduct electricity (shells, erasers, chalk, crayons)

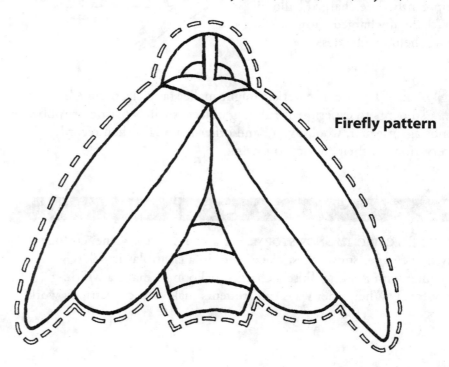

Firefly pattern

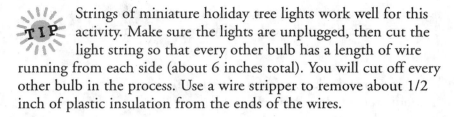

TIP Strings of miniature holiday tree lights work well for this activity. Make sure the lights are unplugged, then cut the light string so that every other bulb has a length of wire running from each side (about 6 inches total). You will cut off every other bulb in the process. Use a wire stripper to remove about 1/2 inch of plastic insulation from the ends of the wires.

1 Guide students to make their fireflies.

- Cut out the firefly pattern. Decorate it with markers, sequins, and other materials.

- Glue the firefly to the flat side of a clothespin, in the center. Let dry.

- Use the clothespin to hold the wired bulb in place on the firefly.

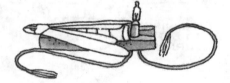

- Tape the plastic-covered ends of the wires to the underside of the firefly's head. These are the firefly's antennae (feelers).

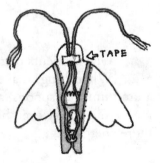

2 Ask: How do you think you can make your firefly light up? Have students explore ways to use the batteries to complete the circuits and make the bulbs light up. To guide them, ask: What has to touch the battery for the bulb to light? What places on the battery need to be touched? (The firefly's feelers—the stripped end of each wire—must come in contact with the top and bottom or negative and positive terminals of the battery. The wires are the conductors of electricity.) Have students draw pictures on their journal pages to show how they made the bulbs light up.

BOOK BREAK

Invite students to find out what really makes fireflies light up. *Fireflies* by Caroline Arnold (Scholastic, 1994) explains how a chemical reaction within a firefly's body creates its signature flash of light and the function this light serves for the insect.

BOOK BREAK

Spark a discussion about how people long ago made light with *Keep the Lights Burning, Abbie* by Peter Roop and Connie Roop (Carolrhoda, 1985), a true story about a girl who, in the days before electricity, keeps a lighthouse going in a storm.

Compare this book with *Arthur's New Power* by Russell Hoban (Harper, 1978), a humorous story about a serious subject, energy conservation. When Arthur, a crocodile, blows one two many fuses, he and his family learn to get along using fewer electrical gadgets.

TIP Have students tape the ends of the wires to the battery terminals if they have difficulty holding them in place.

3 Let students work in pairs to investigate other conductors of electricity. Have them start by taping the end of one feeler to the flat end of the battery and predicting: Besides wire, what other things make good conductors? What else will electricity travel through? Invite students to test their ideas, with one student holding an object against the bumpy end of the battery and the other student touching the end of the other feeler to the object. Does it make the bulb light? Ask students to record predictions and results on the Firefly Tester Chart on their journal pages.

TAPE WIRE → TO BATTERY TERMINAL

4 Give students plenty of time to investigate their ideas, then ask: What things make good conductors? (metal objects such as aluminum foil, spoons, and paper clips) How do you think you could make your firefly even brighter? (Tape on another battery to provide more energy.)

EXTENSION

Morse Code Communicators: Research Morse code and use the fireflies to communicate. Make up new secret codes too.

Crab Legs Puzzler

Students discover that a bulb will light up only when a circuit is complete.

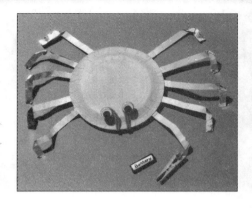

Instead of wires, students use taped foil strips as conductors in this activity. The tape on the strips acts as an insulator. When students use a battery-and-bulb tester to tell which foil strip "crab leg" goes with which, the tape keeps the overlapping strips from conducting electricity to one another. The bulb will light only when the exposed foil ends of the same strip make contact with the battery and bulb, creating a closed circuit.

TIP If you have a limited number of batteries and bulbs, divide students into groups and have them do this activity at different times.

Materials
aluminum foil
3/4- or 1-inch-wide masking tape
ruler
8- or 9-inch paper plates with raised rims (2 per student)
decorating materials (crayons, paints, pipe cleaners, wiggly eyes)
flashlight bulbs (1 per student)
spring-type clothespins (1 per student)
AA batteries (1 per student pair)

1 Demonstrate the steps for making a crab legs puzzler while students follow along.

- Fold the taped foil strips in half length-wise, tape side facing out. Arrange the strips across the inside of one of the plates so that the centers criss-cross and the ends are spaced around the outside of the plate.

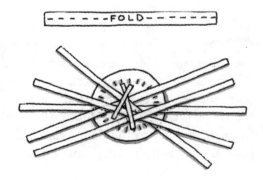

Check that the strips stay folded with the tape side facing out. Tape them to the plate.

To Make Taped Foil Strips

- Lay out about 1 1/2 feet of foil, dull side up.

- Stick strips of 3/4- or 1-inch-wide masking tape side by side, across the length of the foil.

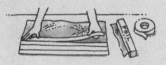

- Separate the strips, laying the edge of a ruler along the edge of a strip of tape and pulling up on the foil so that it tears against the edge of the ruler. Repeat until you have five 18-inch strips for each student.

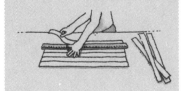

Join the wacky antics of Ms. Frizzle and her class in *The Magic School Bus and the Electric Field Trip* by Joanna Cole and Bruce Degen (Scholastic, 1997). This time the Friz and her class shrink small enough to fit inside a power line and explore how electricity travels and produces energy.

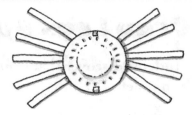

- Place the second plate on top of the plate with the foil strips. Use two small pieces of tape to hold the plates together.

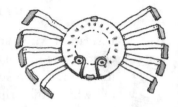

- Unfold the ends of the crab legs (the foil strips) so about 1 1/2 inches of the foil side face out.

- Decorate the plates to look like a crab.

2 Have students swap crabs. Can they tell which leg goes with which without looking inside the plates? Let students work in pairs to make and use battery-and-bulb testers to find out.

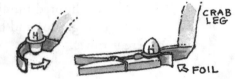

- Wrap one end of a foil strip around a bulb. Use the clothespin to hold the bulb in place.

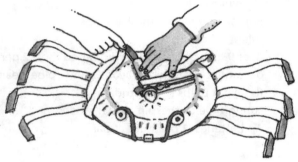

- While one student touches the bottom of the bulb to one end of the battery, the other can touch the end of another foil strip to the other end of the battery. Does the bulb light up? If it does, they've made a match. If not, try another strip. Move the clothespin and bulb setup to another strip to test the rest of the legs.

3 Wrap up by asking students to describe how they made the bulb light up. (The exposed ends of the foil strips are conductors. The bulb lights up when each end of the same strip makes contact with one of the terminals on the battery. Because the end of one of the foil strips is also wrapped around the bulb, it conducts electricity from the battery to the bulb.) Encourage students to explain this process, through drawings and words, in their science journals.

• • • • VARIATION • • • •

LIGHT UP CREATURES: Make other many-legged creatures to light up and test. Octopuses and centipedes are just a couple to try.

Sound

Phones ringing, horns honking, birds singing, children laughing—the world is filled with these and other familiar sounds. Students explore the science behind this form of energy by making simple musical instruments, decorative wind chimes, and more. In the process, they'll learn about sound vibrations—even see how they move!

Buzzing Bee Kazoos

Students make simple kazoos to explore the connection between sound and vibrations.

SCIENCE TALK

All sounds start with *vibrations*—waves that travel through the air or some other medium, such as a solid or a liquid. When students make sounds into their kazoos, the air inside the tubes vibrates. This in turn causes the waxed paper to vibrate. The vibrations then travel through the air, enter their ears, and hit the eardrums, making them vibrate too. From there, the vibrations travel through the middle and inner ear, where they are changed into nerve signals and sent along the auditory nerve to the brain. The brain translates the signals into recognizable sounds.

Materials

waxed paper
scissors
bathroom tissue tubes (1 per student)
rubber bands
pencils
decorating materials such as construction paper scraps, pipe cleaners, markers, paint, crayons
glue

1 Ask students to place their fingers on their throat and say ah-h-h. What do they feel? (a tickle) Explain that the tickle is a vibration. All sounds start with vibrations.

a-a-a-ah

BOOK BREAK

First Science: Making Sounds by Julian Rowe and Molly Perham (Children's Press, 1993) invites readers to explore the science of sound with bright photographs, hands-on activities, and easy-to-understand explanations. Display it at your science center, along with a boxful of materials students need to try the investigations (balloons to explore the way vocal cords work; a sweater, an alarm clock, and a watch that ticks to explore sound waves; and books, rubber bands, and pencils to make stringed instruments). Let children experiment on their own and share discoveries with one another.

2 Invite students to explore other places they can feel vibrations.

- Put a finger on each side of your nose and say n-n-n.

- Press your hand on top of your head and say e-e-e.

- Put your hand on the back of your neck and say ing-ing.

- Press your fingers to your lips and say m-m-m.

3 Have students exaggerate each of the sounds to make them easier to feel. What happens when they make each sound softly, then loudly? (The louder the sound, the stronger the vibration.)

4 Guide students to make kazoos.

- Cut a piece of waxed paper about an inch larger than the tube's opening.

- Cover one end of the tube with waxed paper.

- Stretch a rubber band around the waxed paper to hold it in place. Make sure the waxed paper is smooth and stretched tightly over the opening.

- Use a pencil to poke a hole in the tube (at the end of the tube with the waxed paper).

- Decorate the kazoo to look like a bumblebee. Paint black and yellow stripes on the tube, glue on paper wings, construction paper or wiggly eyes, and add pipe cleaner antennae.

5 Have students hold the open end of their kazoos to their mouths and make some sounds. Can they play a familiar song by humming a tune? As they play, have them touch the waxed paper with their fingers. What do they feel? (a tickle) Have them explore softer and louder sounds as they play.

VARIATIONS

HUM A NEW TUNE: Explore how these changes might affect the sound a kazoo makes.

- Instead of waxed paper, use plastic wrap, aluminum foil, or tissue paper on the end of the kazoos.

- Make longer kazoos with paper towel tubes or gift wrapping tubes.

- Investigate how the sound changes when you cover the holes in the kazoos.

- Make more holes in the kazoo or make them in different places.

EXTENSION

Sound Wigglers: Watch sound vibrations move with this activity.

- Remove both ends of a clean, empty soup can. (Check that there are no sharp edges.) Cut the neck off a balloon. Stretch the balloon over one end of the can so the rubber is smooth and taut. Use a rubber band to hold the balloon in place. Glue sequins or small shapes cut from foil on the balloon.

- Darken the room. Stand in front of a wall and angle a flashlight so it shines on the sequins and foil shapes. Notice the shapes reflected on the wall.

- Talk loudly into the open end of the can while a volunteer shines a flashlight on the shiny shapes. What happens to the reflections? (They move.) What makes them move? (sound vibrations that travel through the can to the balloon) Explore how different kinds of sounds (loud/soft, high/low, singing, humming) change the movement of the reflections.

Songs in the Wind

Students explore the sounds different materials make with wind chimes that capture the music of an outdoor breeze.

SCIENCE TALK

In this activity, students discover that the sounds made by objects on wind chimes vary by their size, shape, and weight. Some objects produce a pure tone when they vibrate. Others produce many different tones and make sounds that are more noise than music. Objects that make high sounds cause the air to vibrate very fast. Those that make low sounds produce slower vibrations.

Materials

variety of wood, plastic, and metal objects (pencils, plastic spoons, old keys, spoons, cookie cutters, O rings, hooks)

yarn or ribbon cut into 12-inch pieces

paper clips

scissors

large paper cups or lightweight plastic or cardboard cereal bowls (1 per student)

pencil

hole punch

assorted art materials such as paint, crayons, markers, glitter, and stickers

1 Display a variety of wood, plastic, and metal objects for students to examine. Ask: What kind of sound do you think each will make on a wind chime?

2 Tie two objects to yarn or ribbon and swing them so they hit each other. Repeat with other objects. Which make musical sounds? (Metal objects produce purer tones because sound vibrations echo within them. Wood and plastic objects absorb vibrations, so they make dull sounds.)

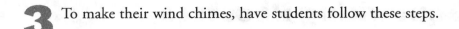

3 To make their wind chimes, have students follow these steps.

- Choose several musical (metal) objects. Tie each to a piece of ribbon or yarn.

- Using a pencil, make a hole in the center of the bottom of a cup. Tie a piece of ribbon or yarn to a paper clip and pull it through the hole inside the cup as shown.

- Punch evenly spaced holes around the rim of the cup, one hole for each object.

- Thread the ribbons, with objects attached, through the holes at the rim and knot each. Try tying the ribbons at different lengths so the metal objects strike one another in a variety of ways.

- Decorate the wind chime with paint, markers, or crayons. Add glitter, stickers, and other decorative items if you like.

4 Help students hang the wind chimes in a breezy spot. Together, listen carefully to the sounds each object makes. Do the sounds change when they hit different objects? How do size, shape, and weight affect an object's sound? Have students record their observations in their science journals.

VARIATION

COOPERATIVE CHIMES: What sounds can you make by attaching a few objects to each piece of ribbon? Let everyone contribute a multiple-object ribbon to make a class wind chime. Use a large plastic juice container, cutting off the bottom and punching holes around the edge to tie on the ribbons.

BOOK BREAK

Poet Arnold Adoff explores the sights, sounds, and rhythms of bustling city life in *Street Music: City Poems* (HarperCollins, 1995). After sharing this collection of poems, take your class on a "sound collection" walk in your neighborhood. Encourage students to focus on the sounds they hear and list them in their science journals. Back in the classroom, invite students to use their lists to write "street music" poems individually or in groups.

Squawking Roosters

Students investigate pitch and volume when they make roosters that squawk!

In this activity, students experiment with factors that affect a sound's *pitch* (highness or lowness) and *volume*. The oatmeal box they use works like the sound box on a guitar or violin. It reinforces the sound vibrations made by the hanging strings, or makes them *resonate*. This happens because the container and the air within it vibrate at the same rate as the strings. The vibrations reinforce each other, creating a louder sound.

When students pull down on the strings with the paper towel, the strings vibrate. They will hear a squeaky sound because sounds travel better through a solid, like string, than they do through air. The thin string makes a higher-pitched sound than the thick string because it vibrates more rapidly. Pitch is also affected by the length of the strings and the tension applied to them. Why do the wet strings make even louder sounds? The moisture makes them vibrate more easily, compressing more of the surrounding air and increasing the volume of the sound they produce.

Materials

small cylinder-shaped boxes, without covers, such as oatmeal boxes
   (1 per student)
pencils
rulers
thick cotton string
thin cotton string (button thread works well)
paper clips
tape
assorted art supplies (construction paper, wiggly eyes, craft feathers)
scissors
paper towels
water

1 Have students use a sharp pencil to make two holes in the bottom of the box, positioned as shown.

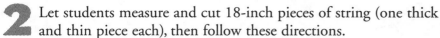

2 Let students measure and cut 18-inch pieces of string (one thick and thin piece each), then follow these directions.

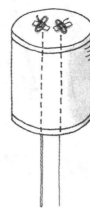

- Tie a paper clip to one end of each string.

- Use a pencil point to poke the other end of each string through the holes in the bottom of the box.

- Tape the paper clips to the bottom of the box. When the box is turned right side up, the strings will hang down.

3 Invite students to decorate their boxes to look like roosters, for example, by covering them with construction paper, then adding wiggly eyes, a paper beak, craft feather wings, and a tail.

4 Have students investigate the kinds of sounds their roosters can make. Give them each a paper towel folded into quarters and demonstrate how to gently squeeze it around the thin string and pull it down, then repeat with the thick string. Ask students to compare the sounds each string makes in their science journals. (The thin string makes a higher-pitched sound than the thick string because it vibrates more rapidly.)

5 Have students wet the strings and repeat step 4. How do the sounds change? (All of the sounds are louder and sharper; the thin string still makes a higher-pitched sound; the thick string makes a low-pitched one). Ask students to record their observations.

6 Invite students to experiment making sounds in different ways (pull down on the string in a start-and-stopping motion, pull down to make prolonged squawks, and so on).

· · · · · · VARIATION · · · · · · · ·

SOUND TEST: Experiment with containers of different sizes or materials (plastic or foam cups, yogurt containers) and strings of different thickness (yarn, dental floss, regular thread). How do the sounds compare?

BOOK BREAK

The Voice of the Wood by Claude Clément (Dial, 1989). Evocative paintings illustrate this mystical tale of an instrument maker and a cello he creates from the wood of a magnificent old tree—a tree that gives the cello strength from its wood and sweet songs from the birds in its branches.

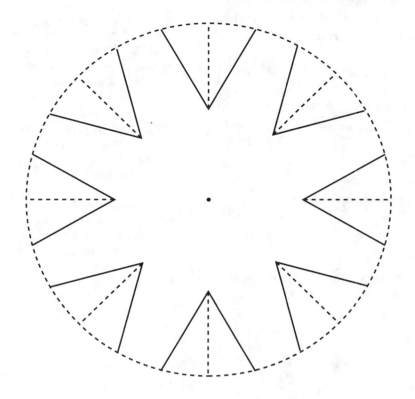

Warm Air Whirler
▲▲▲▲▲

Pinwheel
▲▲▲▲▲

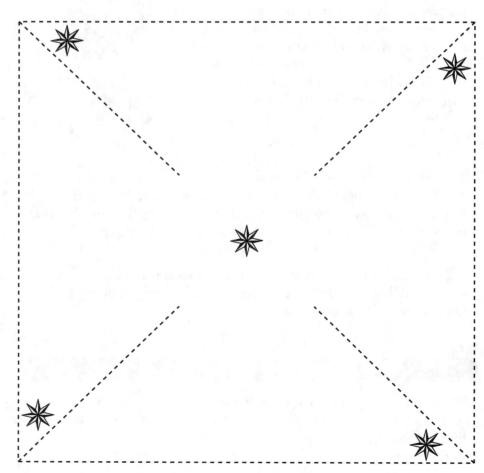

Flashing Firefly

1. Draw a picture that shows how you made your firefly light up.

Firefly Tester Chart

Objects I Tested	Will It Make the Firefly Light Up?	
	My Prediction	**My Results**

Forces & Movement

What holds us on Earth and keeps us from toppling over when we walk? What makes seesaws balance and magnets push and pull? With the projects in this chapter, students investigate forces that make things balance and move.

Gravity

There's no easy definition of gravity, but with the activities here students will experience this force as they watch what happens when drops of colored water splash down on paper, and make toy clowns and mobiles balance.

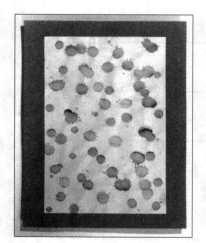

Splish-Splash Paintings

How does gravity affect falling objects? Students make drop paintings to find out.

▲▲▲▲▲▲▲▲▲▲▲▲▲▲▲▲▲▲▲
SCIENCE TALK
▼▼▼▼▼▼▼▼▼▼▼▼▼▼▼▼▼▼▼

Gravity is the force that pulls all objects downward—and holds us on Earth. (A force is anything that pushes or pulls on an object. A push or pull can change an object's speed or direction of motion.) In this activity, drops of paint that fall from a greater height travel faster so they hit the paper with more force and make a bigger splash.

Materials

newspaper
plastic cups (3 per group)
water
food coloring
eyedroppers or straws (3 per group)
craft paper
Splish-Splash Paintings journal page (page 131)
scissors
smocks

TIP If you use straws instead of eyedroppers, let students practice picking up and dropping water.

1 Divide students into small groups. Have each group set up a work area by spreading newspaper on the floor. Prepare three paint cups for each group by mixing water with different food colorings. Put an eyedropper or straw into each cup.

2 Place a sheet of craft paper on the newspaper for each student in a group. Give everyone a Splish-Splash Paintings journal page.

3 Ask students to test the effect of dropping paint from different heights.

- Predict and draw on the chart the size splash the drop will make if you hold the dropper at shoulder height. Release a drop. Observe the splash size. Label this splash "shoulder height."

- Predict and record the size splash a drop will make if you hold the dropper at waist height, then at knee height. Each time, use a different color of paint and hold the dropper over a different place on the paper. Let a drop fall from each height, observe the splash size, and label.

4 When the splashes dry, have students cut them out and paste them onto their charts, then compare predictions with results. Ask: Did your predictions get more accurate each time you tried a new drop? Do drops that fall from higher up make splashes that are bigger or smaller? (bigger) Can students explain why?

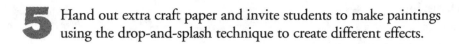

5 Hand out extra craft paper and invite students to make paintings using the drop-and-splash technique to create different effects.

Balancing Clowns

Students explore center of gravity to make clowns balance on their fingertips!

S C I E N C E   T A L K

Since gravity pulls everything downward, why don't we fall down? Our muscles help us stand up straight against gravity's force. And the floor pushes upward to stop our fall. In addition, all objects have a balancing point or *center of gravity.* In this activity, to balance the clown on a fingertip, its weight must be spread evenly around this point. Placing paper clips near the bottom of each of the clown's hands lowers the center of gravity, helping to stabilize the clown and make it balance.

Materials
3 yardsticks
masking tape
heavy book
Balancing Clown pattern page (page 132)
thin cardboard
glue
scissors
paper clips
pencils

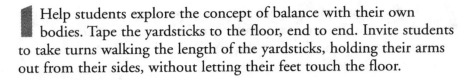

1 Help students explore the concept of balance with their own bodies. Tape the yardsticks to the floor, end to end. Invite students to take turns walking the length of the yardsticks, holding their arms out from their sides, without letting their feet touch the floor.

2 Then have students try walking the length of the yardsticks with these variations.

- Cross your arms over your chest.

- Hold a heavy book in one hand, with that arm held out to one side.

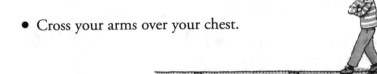

- Hold the book with both hands, below your waist, close to your body.

3 Discuss results. Which method was easiest? Hardest? (Holding their arms out is easiest because this redistributes some of students' body weight, allowing them to compensate for weight shifts on the beam. It's harder to balance with arms crossed. Holding the book in one hand throws the body off-balance because the center of gravity moves to one side. But holding the book close to the body lowers the center of gravity and keeps it over the feet, also making it easier to balance.)

4 Hand out the Balancing Clown pattern. Have students glue the page to cardboard, then cut out their clowns.

5 Challenge students to balance their clowns by the head on their fingertip or on the end of a pencil. Can they do it? (no)

BOOK BREAK

As students explore their own balancing abilities, introduce them to Henry, the resourceful cat in *High-Wire Henry* by Mary Calhoun (Morrow, 1991), who waves his tail and spreads his whiskers to balance on a fence. How will Henry use his balancing know-how to save a puppy stuck on a window ledge?

For another look at balancing, share *Mirette on the High Wire* by Emily Arnold McCully (Putnam, 1992). Set in Paris in the 1800s, this is the story of a young girl who longs to walk the high wire, just like the world-famous Bellini.

6 Explain that by adding weight (the paper clips) somewhere on the clowns, students can make them balance. Ask students to predict where they should place the paper clips. Have them sketch ideas in their science journals.

7 Invite students to test their predictions. Have them place the paper clips on their clowns, then set them on their fingers. Were their predictions correct? If not, have them move the paper clips around until the clowns balance.

8 Have students draw pictures in their science journals showing how they made their clowns balance. Discuss the best place to add weight to the clowns (two or more paper clips on each hand, to evenly distribute the weight and to offset the force pulling down on the clown's body and legs). Then invite students to investigate: What effect does adding extra weight have? Follow up by discussing ways balance helps us in everyday life (for example, riding bikes and skateboards).

● ● ● **V A R I A T I O N** ● ● ●

TIGHTROPE TRICK: Balance clowns on a tightrope. (Tie a string across one corner of your classroom.) Try designing other balancing toys too.

● ● ● **E X T E N S I O N** ● ● ●

Help Humpty Dumpty: Experiment with making eggs that keep their balance—instead of falling over. You'll need plastic Easter eggs, tape, glue, and materials to weight the eggs, such as sand, salt, plasticine, pebbles, or pennies. Wiggly eyes, felt, and other materials are fun for decorating the eggs.

- Investigate answers to these questions: Does adding weight to the inside or the outside of the egg keep it from tipping over? To the narrow end or the wider end of the egg? How much weight works best?

- Experiment with different solutions, then share methods that worked as well as those that didn't. (By adding weight to the egg's wider end, you can create a wider, more stable base and lower the egg's center of gravity. Adding the weight *inside* the egg lets Humpty Dumpty rock but not fall down.)

Starry Sky Mobiles

Students investigate balance by making mobiles that sparkle and shine like a starry night sky.

To balance mobiles in this activity, students adjust the position of the center of gravity, spreading the weight of the shapes and straws evenly around this point. How can a small shape balance a larger one?

Think of a mobile as a collection of suspended seesaws. A seesaw moves about on a center pivot point called a *fulcrum*. A heavier child close to the center balances a lighter child sitting farther out. In the mobiles students make, each straw pivots on its paper clip chain. Placing a light weight farther from the fulcrum balances a heavier one positioned closer to the fulcrum.

Materials
colored tagboard
scissors
glue
glitter
hole punch
small paper clips (colored ones make a great effect)
rulers
tape
straws (4 per student)
string

1 Have students cut out six night sky shapes from the tagboard (crescents, half moons, star shapes, and so on). To help them explore the effect of balancing different weights, have students make three smaller shapes and three larger ones (up to about 4 inches across works well). Then invite them to decorate the shapes with glue and glitter and punch a hole near the edge of each shape.

2 Show students how to make paper clip chains using two paper clips for each chain. Have students hook each shape to a chain, then construct their mobiles.

 Paper clip chains are easy for students to lengthen or shorten. However, you can substitute pieces of string cut to different lengths.

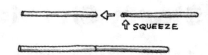

- Squeeze one end of a straw and slip it into another straw to make a longer straw.

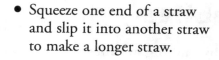

- Make a long paper clip chain using about six paper clips. Hang it from the center of the long straw. (Attach the smaller end of the paper clip to the straw to keep the chain from sliding off.)

TIP Set up work areas for students. You might stretch a length of string across a corner of your classroom so several students can work on their mobiles at the same time. Or have students each tape a ruler to the edge of their desk with the ruler extending over the floor. Students can then tape their mobiles-in-progress to the end of the ruler.

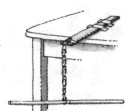

- Make two more chains, one longer than the other. Attach each chain to a straw. Then hook two shapes to each straw by their chains as shown.

- Hang these two setups from the long straw, moving them until they balance.

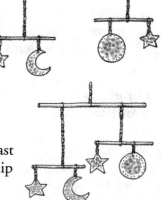

- Pick a spot on the mobile to hang the last two shapes (already attached to paper clip chains), making adjustments so they balance.

3 Invite students to share ways they made their mobiles balance. Do all of the mobiles arrangements look the same? (Setups may vary depending on where students decided to hang the shapes.) What would happen if students removed one of the shapes or if they combined two mobiles? Would the mobiles still balance? Challenge students to test their ideas.

4 Display mobiles from the ceiling using string and tape.

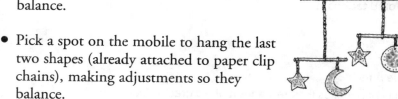

VARIATION

MORE MOBILES: Students can substitute the iridescent paper from the Shimmery Color Bursts activity (see page 81) for the colored tagboard. Instead of night sky shapes, they might balance their Crystal Creations (see page 57) or their Warm Air Whirlers (see page 99), or they can make mobiles that relate to other topics of study such as life cycles, weather, or plants.

Magnets

In this set of activities, students experiment with magnetic forces. They find out how magnets can both attract and repel and discover that a magnet's force extends beyond the magnet itself.

Magnetic Force Faces

Students use magnetic force to draw features on faces.

SCIENCE TALK

Why do magnets attract only certain metals? Magnets, and the metals they attract (iron, steel, nickel, and cobalt), contain groups of atoms that align and face the same direction. These aligned atoms produce a magnetic attraction. When a metal object comes in contact with a magnet, its atoms line up with the magnet's magnetic field and make the metal a temporary magnet. A magnet's force exists not only within the magnet, but also extends beyond it. That's why a magnet can attract a piece of metal without touching it.

Materials

steel-mesh pot-scrubbing pads (not the steel wool kind containing cleanser) or iron filings
plastic bag
old scissors
rubber gloves
assorted magnetic and nonmagnetic objects (paper clips, buttons, aluminum foil, erasers, nails, candles, wood blocks)
magnets (see Supply Sources, page 9) (1 per student)
Magnetic Force Faces pattern page (page 133)
clear plastic clamshell containers or other take-out containers with clear plastic lids (8-by-9-inch size works well) (1 per student)
tape
glue

SAFETY NOTE

Use magnets with care around computer software, videos, and credit cards because they can damage these materials. Also, encourage students to handle magnets gently. Striking a magnet against a hard object can reduce its strength.

1 Prepare for this activity by cutting up the pot-scrubbing pads into tiny pieces. (Put the pads in a plastic bag and wear rubber gloves. Use old scissors to cut up the pads inside the bag.) Or use iron filings available from science supply companies (see Supply Sources, page 9).

2 Divide students into groups. Give each group a bag of magnetic and nonmagnetic objects along with a magnet for each student. Ask students to predict and record in their science journals which objects will stick to the magnet and which will not.

3 Let students test the objects, then bring the class together to share results. (Objects made of iron or steel stick to the magnets. Nonmetal objects and metal objects made of aluminum, copper, or silver do not.)

4 Hand out plastic containers, scissors, magnets, tape, and copies of the Magnetic Force Faces pattern. Enlarge or reduce the pattern to fit the size of your containers. Guide students in setting them up.

- Place the container on top of the face on the pattern page, trace around it, then cut it out and glue it inside the container, face up.

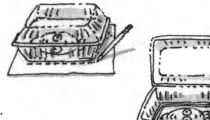

- Pour a few teaspoons of the metal pieces into the container (adult only). Tell students not to touch the metal pieces. Close the cover and seal the container with tape.

5 Tell students to move their magnets under the containers. What happens? (The magnet's force goes through the container and the metal pieces move around with the magnet.) Invite students to use their magnets to make hair, eyes, and other features on the faces. What happens when they remove the magnet and shake the container gently? (The metal pieces scatter.)

 TIP For added fun, have students turn their containers around. What happens? They now have a different face to put features on!

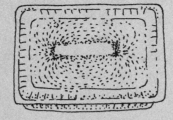

Magnetic Field Finders: Explore the lines of force around a magnet.

- Instead of the Magnetic Force Faces pattern, put a piece of plain white paper inside the container. Then place a magnet underneath and observe how the metal pieces line up. This pattern shows how far the magnet's force extends and where the force is strongest (where the metal pieces are the most concentrated) and weakest.

- Place two magnets of the same type under the container so that their unlike poles face each other, then so their like poles face each other. Observe the patterns that form.

- Experiment with different kinds of magnets (ring, horseshoe, bar, U-shaped) and their lines of force.

Jumping Kangaroos

Students explore magnetic repulsion by making kangaroos that jump!

S C I E N C E   T A L K

Every magnet has a north and south pole where the magnet's powers are strongest. Opposite poles (north and south) attract or pull together, and like poles (north/north, south/south) repel or push away from each other.

Materials

ring or latch magnets with holes (at least 2 per student) (see Supply Sources, page 9)

coffee stirrers or pencils (1 per student)

3-ounce paper cups (1 per student)

kangaroo pattern (page 128)

scissors

glue or tape

1 Give each student two magnets. After allowing time to explore, ask: What are some things you discovered about the magnets? (Sometimes they stick together; sometimes they push away from each other.) Discuss the concept of opposite and like poles. (See Science Talk, above.) Ask students where they think the poles of a ring magnet are. (on the top and bottom of the ring)

2 Challenge students to make the magnets stick together on a coffee stirrer or pencil. Can they make the magnets push apart or float on the stick? When everyone's magnets are floating, ask students to try to push the two magnets together. How does it feel? (You feel the magnetic force resisting.)

TIP Coffee stirrers work well with latch magnets, which have small holes. For ring magnets with larger holes, use pencils.

3 Show students how to apply what they learned to make high-jumping kangaroos.

- Use the pencil or coffee stirrer to poke a hole in the middle of the bottom of a paper cup. The pencil or stirrer should move easily through the hole.

- Line up the hole in one of the magnets with the hole in the bottom of the cup. Glue or tape the magnet to the bottom of the cup.

- Cut out the kangaroo pattern and glue it to the side of the cup.

- Slide the other magnet onto the pencil (or stirrer), then slide the cup on top. If the magnets stick together, flip the magnet on the pencil. (The pencil or stirrer keeps the magnets aligned.)

- Hold the pencil or stirrer in one hand and push down gently on the cup with the other. Watch the kangaroo jump!

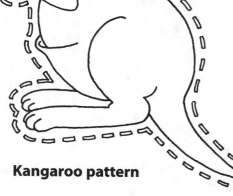

Kangaroo pattern

4 As students play with their toys, ask them to explain what is happening. (When like poles of two magnets are facing each other, the magnets push apart or repel.) Ask: How can you make the kangaroos jump even higher? (Use more magnets.) Hand out extras and invite students to test their ideas. Observe how well they apply what they learned about magnetic attraction and repulsion earlier in the activity.

● ● ● **VARIATION** ● ● ●

MOVE IT WITH MAGNETS: Use what you learned about magnetic repulsion in Jumping Kangaroos to make other animals move. For example, can you make bats that flap and flutter or bunnies hop?

High-Flying Birds

Students make birds fly high as they discover that a magnet's force extends beyond the magnet itself.

SCIENCE TALK

In this activity, the bird flies because the magnet's force passes through air to attract the paper clip taped to the bird, overcoming the pull of gravity. If students carefully place nonmagnetic materials such as aluminum foil, paper, or plastic between the bird and the magnet, the bird will still fly because a magnet's force passes through these materials. However, any magnetic materials, such as another paper clip or a nail, will disturb the magnetic field and cause the bird to fall.

Materials (for each student)
bird pattern (right)
scissors
thread
rulers
paper clips
tape
strong magnet (or several weak magnets stacked together)

Bird pattern

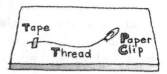

BOOK BREAK

For an unusual look at magnetism, share *Home in the Sky* by Jeannie Baker (Greenwillow, 1984), a gentle story about a homing pigeon that has a variety of adventures in the city before finding its way home. Explain to students that scientists believe homing pigeons get their acute sense of direction from magnetic crystals within their bodies that work like a compass to help them navigate.

1 Give students copies of the bird pattern to cut out. Have them make their birds "fly."

- Tie one end of a 12-inch-long piece of thread to a paper clip. Tape the other end to your desk.

- Tape the paper clip to the bird.

- Use a magnet to pick up the bird. Lift the bird until the thread is straight. Gently pull the magnet away from the bird to make it fly.

2 Ask: What do you think would happen if you put something between the bird and the magnet? Would your bird still fly? Challenge students to find out by testing paper, plastic, wood, or other metal objects. Have them record their findings in their science journals.

EXTENSIONS

Refrigerator Magnets: Roll out air-drying clay to about 1/4 inch thickness. Cut into shapes and let dry. (Use cookie cutters for fun.) Paint and decorate with sequins, feathers, seeds, wiggly eyes, or other materials. Glue a small magnet to the back of each.

Magnet Race Mazes: Design mazes on thin cardboard. Make simple standing cardboard figures (with paper clips taped to flaps on their feet). To play, hold a magnet beneath the maze and pull the figures through.

Magnetic Dancers: Make simple figures out of pipe cleaners, bending the legs to form flat feet and sliding a paper clip onto each. Place the figures on a paper plate. Make the figures stand up and dance around by moving the magnet underneath.

Name _____

Splish-Splash Paintings

	Predicted Splash Size	Actual Splash Size
Drop 1 (drop from shoulder height)		
Drop 2 (drop from waist height)		
Drop 3 (drop from knee height)		

Think About It: What if you used thicker kinds of paint?
How might the size of your splashes change?

ScienceART Scholastic Professional Books

Balancing Clown

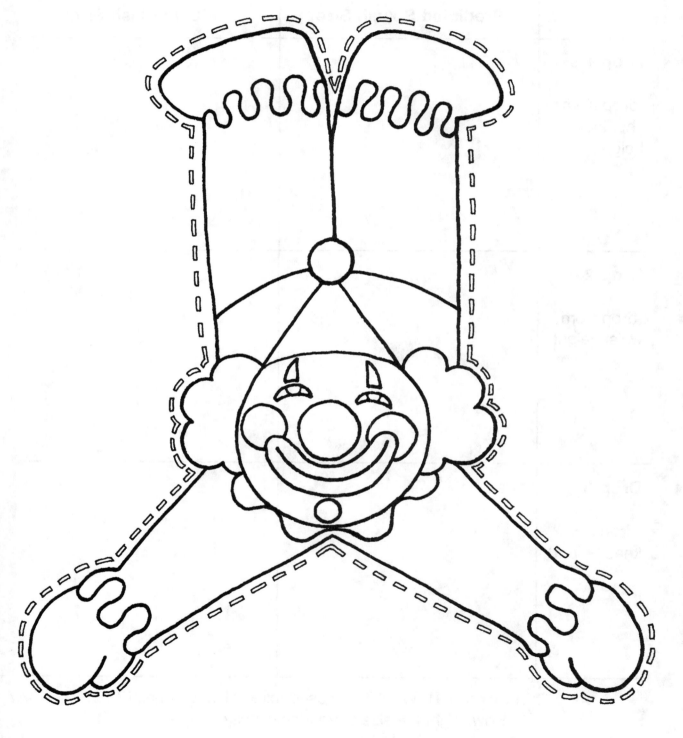

Magnetic Force Faces

The Way Liquids Work

From marbleized oil-and-water pictures to colorful, layered liquid rainbows, the activities in this chapter invite students to investigate the properties of liquids and objects that sink and float. In the process, they'll build a foundation for understanding cohesion, density, surface tension, and other scientific concepts.

Cohesion at Work

Introduce students to the concept of *cohesion*—the force that causes things like water molecules to stick together—by letting them play with drops of oil and water on waxed paper. First, have students observe how each drop looks. (The oil drop is flat and spread out. The water drop is higher and rounder.) Next, have them perform the following tests and record their observations.

- Add three drops of oil to the first drop of oil. Add three drops of water to the first drop of water. (The drops of oil don't clump together as tightly as water droplets do. Oil drops tend to spread out more than the water.)

- Use the tip of the dropper to pull away on the water. Do the same thing with the oil. Can you move oil drops the same way as water drops? (No. Oil drops smear while water drops stay in a clump and can be pulled across the paper.)

- Try mixing the drops of oil with the drops of water. Can you separate them again? (Students will discover that they cannot mix the oil and water. To separate the drops, they can simply tip the waxed paper. The water will move away from the oil.)

Bring students together to summarize their observations about the properties of oil and water. (Water drops are higher and rounder and clump together more than do oil drops. That's because water is more cohesive—when two or more droplets are near enough to each other, they join together. Also, oil and water drops don't mix.)

Marbleized Paper Pictures

Oil and water don't mix—but in this activity they team up to create beautiful marbleized designs.

▲▲▲▲▲▲▲▲▲▲▲▲▲▲▲▲▲▲▲▲▲▲▲▲▲▲▲▲▲▲▲▲▲▲▲▲▲

SCIENCE TALK

In this activity, the tempera-and-oil paint floats on top of the water because oil is less dense than water. (See Science Talk, page 139, for more about density.) Water and oil are also *immiscible*, meaning they do not dissolve into each other. The reason? Substances are either *polar* (like water) or *nonpolar* (like most oils). The molecules of polar substances move easily between one another (such as when tea leaves or food coloring infuse in water). The molecules of nonpolar substances do not. Polar and nonpolar substances do not form solutions.

Materials

newspaper
paper cups
powdered tempera paints
cooking oil
plastic spoons
plastic wrap
disposable foil baking pan
water
toothpicks
white paper
paper towels
smocks

1 Cover a work surface with newspaper. Make the paint ahead of time: Put a few spoonfuls of powdered tempera paint in a cup. Mix in a spoonful of oil. The mixture should be the consistency of maple syrup. Prepare a few different colors of paint in separate cups. Cover them with plastic wrap until ready to use.

2 Fill the pan halfway with water. Show students how to hold a spoonful of paint close to the water's surface, then carefully and slowly let it fall, drop by drop onto the water.

3 Let students swirl the different colors of paint with toothpicks.

4 To make marbleized paper, let students take turns laying their paper on top of the paint in the water, gently tapping the paper to cover the entire surface. Then have students lift the paper by the edges and place on paper towels to dry. If the papers curl as they dry, place them facedown under a heavy book. Students can apply this technique to make marbleized bookmarks, book covers, paper picture frames, note cards (fold unlined index cards in half and dip one side into the marbling mixture), envelopes, and gift bags and wrap.

TIP Wipe up excess paint from the pan with newspaper or paper towels. When you pour the water down the drain, let the hot water run a bit to make sure oil residue does not clog the drain.

VARIATIONS

TRY A NEW TOOL: Experiment with using plastic forks, feathers, and other tools to make swirly designs in the paint.

CRAYON-SHAVING SWIRLS: Substitute crayon shavings for the paint-and-oil mixture. Fill the pan with very hot water and sprinkle crayon shavings over the surface. The heat of the water will melt the crayon. Swirl with a toothpick and lay the paper on the water.

EXTENSION

Nature's Own: Learn about natural marble, a kind of metamorphic rock formed through heat and extreme pressure. Compare marbleized paper designs with those in this unusual kind of stone.

Drifting Drops

Students will be spellbound by these liquid-filled jars—and at the same time will begin to build an understanding of two difficult concepts, surface tension and density.

SCIENCE TALK

What happens when water droplets fall into oil? They form almost perfect spheres because of the high *surface tension*—or low attraction—between oil and water. The water molecules are cohesive—they pull in toward one another to form a sphere, the shape that takes up the least possible surface area in the oil. Because water is more dense than oil, the water drops sink. But by tipping the jar in different ways, students can keep the drops suspended in the oil. When the jar is kept still, the drops flatten out on the bottom. Shaking breaks up the drops into many tiny droplets. (See Science Talk, page 139 for more about density.)

Materials

measuring spoons
water
cup
food coloring
eyedroppers or straws
small glass jars with lids (baby food jars work well) (1 per student)
mineral or cooking oil, enough to fill the jars

Make a Drifting Drops jar ahead of time.

- Put 1 tablespoon of water in a cup. Mix in three drops of food coloring.

- Fill a jar almost to the top with oil.

- Add two or three drops of colored water to the oil. (Don't touch the dropper to the oil.)

- Put the lid on the jar.

COLORED WATER

OIL

After comparing the properties of water with other liquids, students will be fascinated by Walter Wick's *A Drop of Water* (Scholastic, 1997). Spectacular close-up photos show water in its various states—as droplets falling and splashing, steam, snowflakes, and ice. Clear accompanying text explains the science behind each photo.

For different poets' perspectives on the properties of water and rain, share *Rainy Day Rhymes* (Houghton Mifflin, 1992), a collection of 17 poems selected by Gail Radley.

2 Show students the Drifting Drops jar and ask them what they think is inside. Encourage them to think about what they learned in the previous activity.

3 Next, guide students in making their own Drifting Drops jars. (You may want to have students work in groups, sharing one jar per group.) Ask: What happens to the drops when they hit the oil? (They form ball shapes, or spheres.)

4 Tell students to put the lids on their jars and close them tightly. Have them gently tip the jars in different ways. Ask: What happens to the colored drops? (They float slowly through the oil and eventually sink.)

5 Invite students to shake the jars. What happens to the drops? (They break up, forming many smaller spheres.) Have students record observations in their science journals.

● ● ● ● **V A R I A T I O N S** ● ● ● ●

TRY A NEW LIQUID: Instead of adding drops of colored water to oil, use rubbing alcohol mixed with a few drops of food coloring. Notice how drops of alcohol behave in the oil compared to drops of water. (The drops of alcohol are less dense than water so they float longer in the oil.)

REVERSE THE PROCEDURE: Substitute colored water for oil in the jar then add a few drops of oil to the water. What happens?

Layered Liquid Rainbows

Students explore the density of different liquids as they make unusual rainbows.

∆∆∆∆∆∆∆∆∆∆∆∆∆∆∆∆∆∆∆∆∆∆∆∆∆∆∆ S C I E N C E T A L K ∆∆∆∆∆∆∆∆∆∆∆∆∆∆∆∆∆∆∆∆∆∆∆

Why do some liquids float on top of others? In this activity, students discover the answer—density. Density measures how heavy something is for the space it takes up. For example, of the four liquids students investigate in this activity, corn syrup is the most dense, and rubbing alcohol is the least. In other words, a cup of corn syrup weighs more than a cup of alcohol. Less dense liquids float in more dense ones. The layered effect in this activity is achieved by using four liquids with different densities.

Materials
measuring cup
light corn syrup
corn oil
water
rubbing alcohol
paper cups (4 per group)
food coloring (blue, red, green)
tall, clear plastic tumblers (1 per group)
plastic spoons (3 per group)
Layered Liquid Rainbows journal page (page 144)
crayons or markers

1 Divide students into groups for this activity. For each group, place 1/4 cup of each liquid in separate paper cups. Mix a few drops of food coloring into three of the liquids as follows (leave the oil uncolored): red—corn syrup, blue—water, and green—alcohol. This will help keep the identity of the liquids a secret as well as distinguish the different layers and create a beautiful effect.

TIP Before starting this project, you might want to have students explore the properties of each of the liquids. (See Cohesion at Work, page 134.)

2 Give each group a set of cups filled with the liquids, a clear tumbler, three plastic spoons, and a journal page for each student. Demonstrate how to make a layered liquid rainbow.

SAFETY NOTE

 Remind students that, like scientists, they should not taste any of the materials they are experimenting with. Though the corn syrup, oil, and water in this activity are harmless, rubbing alcohol is dangerous if ingested.

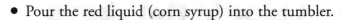

- Pour the red liquid (corn syrup) into the tumbler.

- Add the blue liquid (water), holding a plastic spoon inside the glass. (Don't touch the spoon to the red liquid.) Carefully pour the blue water onto the spoon, so it drips a little bit at a time on top of the red liquid.

- Using a fresh plastic spoon for each liquid, add the yellow liquid (oil), then the green liquid (alcohol) in the same way.

3 Ask students to observe what happens as they add each liquid to the glass. (Each liquid floats in a layer on top of the previous layer.) Have them draw and label pictures of their observations on their journal pages. Can they guess what each liquid is?

4 Bring students together to share observations. Discuss the properties of each liquid and record students' guesses about what each liquid might be. Ask them to explain how the liquids float on top of one another. (Students may say that the liquids on top are lighter than the liquids on the bottom of the glass. This is a simple and age-appropriate explanation of density, which will lay the foundation for a more detailed understanding in later grades. See Science Talk, page 139.)

• • • • V A R I A T I O N S • • • •

SINK OR FLOAT: Predict and test what will happen if you drop a few small objects such as plastic beads, corks, or birthday candles in the glass. Which will float? Which will sink? If they float, what layer will they land in?

STIR IT UP: What will happen to the liquids if you stir them up with a spoon? Will they separate into layers again? Test to find out.

LAYER OTHER LIQUIDS: Experiment with layering other liquids such as molasses, maple syrup, honey, dishwashing liquid, shampoo, vinegar, and salt water. Compare with the original four.

PAPERWEIGHT PRESENTS: Make layered rainbows in jars with straight sides and tight-fitting lids. Wrap up these liquid-filled paperweights for gifts.

Sink & Float Sparkle Jars

Make jars that sparkle and swirl to explore the effect of mixing liquids, solids, and gases of different densities.

SCIENCE TALK

In this activity, liquids and objects of different densities create a mesmerizing effect in a jar. Filling the jar with a viscous corn syrup–and–water mixture allows glitter and sequins to swirl around slowly, staying suspended longer than if placed in water alone. (In water, the glitter and sequins swirl quickly, then rapidly sink.) An air bubble in the jar, less dense than any of the other substances in the jar, floats to the top.

Materials

tall, narrow jars with lids (such as those that some olives, jam, or Tabasco sauce come in) (1 per student)

glitter, small plastic sequins, bits of tinsel, crayon shavings, seed beads (see Tip, below)

water

light corn syrup

cardboard

tape

waxed paper

2 eyedroppers

food coloring (optional)

ribbon (optional)

 Make two jars ahead of time. Fill one jar (up to 1/2 inch below the rim) with water, the other with half water and half corn syrup. Add a pinch or two of glitter or sequins to each jar. Put the lid on each jar and close tightly.

TIP For jars with narrow openings, roll a piece of paper into a cone and use it like a funnel to get sequins and glitter in more easily. Instead of sequins, you can use a hole punch to cut out dots from colored plastic report covers.

2 Help students investigate corn syrup's *viscosity*—resistance to flow. Cover a piece of cardboard with waxed paper and tilt it. Use eyedroppers to put a drop each of corn syrup and water at the top of the cardboard. (Ask a volunteer to hold the cardboard so you can place both drops on at the same time.) Have students observe and compare the speed of the drops as they move down the cardboard. (The corn syrup moves more slowly than the water.)

3 Pass around the jars. Without shaking them, ask students what they observe inside each jar. (a liquid; solids—glitter and sequins that swirl through the liquid, then sink; a gas—an air bubble that rises to the top)

4 Hold up the jars. Then turn them upside down. Ask students to look carefully at the movement of objects inside and guess what the liquids might be. (The objects in the corn syrup–and–water jar move more slowly than those in the jar with water only.)

5 Guide students in making their own jars, following the directions for corn syrup–and–water given in step 1. They can add a drop of food coloring to the jars if they wish or tie on colorful ribbons around the cap.

6 Invite students to observe the behavior of the solids, liquids, and gas inside their jars. Use these questions to guide their explorations.

- What happens when you twirl the jar in a circle? (A mini-whirlpool forms.)

- Where does the air bubble go? (It moves around when the jar is tipped but goes back to the top of the jar when the jar is still.)

- Which objects float? Which sink? How long does it take them to sink? Use a watch with a second hand to time them. Why do you think some sink more quickly? (See Science Talk, page 141.)

- Based on what you've observed, what other objects do you think will sink? Which ones will sink first? Let students make new jars to test their ideas.

E X T E N S I O N

Sink & Float Snow Globes: You'll need wide-mouthed jars with lids (baby food jars work well), a hot-glue gun (or florist's clay), glitter, small plastic figures or objects to glue inside the jars (plastic cake decorations work well).

- Use the hot-glue gun (adult only) to glue one or two plastic figures inside the lid. Let the glue harden. (Or place a bit of florist's clay on the inside of the lid. Press figures into the clay.)

- Pour water into the jar until it is almost full.

- Sprinkle glitter into the jar.

- Put on the lid and close it tightly.

- Shake your snow globe. Watch the snow swirl through the water, then sink.

Name _____

Layered Liquid Rainbows

1. Draw a picture of your layered liquid rainbow.

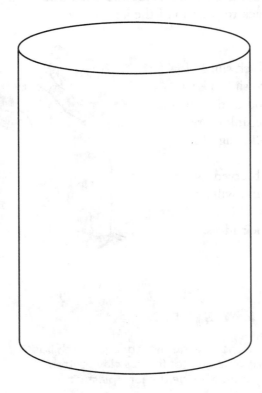

2. Can you guess the name of each liquid?

	My Guess	**Actual Name**
Green		
Yellow		
Blue		
Red		

ScienceART • Scholastic Professional Books